Professional
LEADERSHIP

International leadership professionals
share their current best thinking on
how to lead cultural transformation
to enhance business outcomes

WM

Professional Leadership

First published in November 2022
WM Publishing

ISBN 978-1-914265-34-1 Ebk
ISBN 978-1-914265-35-8 Pbk

Editors: Angela Armstrong PhD and Andrew Priestley

The rights of MPI Learning; and Angela Armstrong PhD, Maggi Evans PhD, James Hall, Andy Goram, Nick Corbo, Ellen Burton, Vanessa Boon, Susan Croft, Matthew Storey, Fraser Murray to be identified as contributing authors of this work have been asserted in accordance with Sections 77 and 78 of the Copyright Designs and Patents Act, 1988.

A CIP catalogue record for this book is available from the British Library.

Disclaimer: *Professional Leadership* is intended for information and education purposes only. This book does not constitute specific advice unique to your situation. While this book mentions the terms Covid, Coronavirus and pandemic, this book does NOT contain medical, clinical, treatment or pharmaceutical advice.

All people mentioned in case studies have been used with permission, and/or have had names, genders, industries and personal details altered to protect client confidentiality. Any resemblance to persons living or dead is purely coincidental.

To the best of our knowledge, the Publisher and Authors have complied with fair usage. The Publisher will be glad to rectify all future editions if omissions are bought to their attention.

www.mpilearning.com

https://mpilearning.com/contact-us/

Contents

Leading Yourself

Welcome

Angela Armstrong PhD

I am so excited to deliver you this book, at this moment.

There are enormous challenges facing us globally, organisationally and personally right now. Despite the pressures, I know that there are many leaders amongst us who are positive role models, who are resourceful in finding solutions and, who are forever curious about how they can be a better leader day by day. *Are you that leader?* Someone with the audacity to envision a brighter future, the courage and capability to make it happen and the passion to inspire others to help? Someone who understands the responsibility that comes with having far-reaching impact on people's daily lives and livelihoods, regardless of what's going on in your own?

Are you a leader who can be relied upon to deliver measurable business outcomes, and do so in a way that treats people like the free-willed, creative and compassionate individuals they are? Leadership is approximately 20% science and 80% art; two leaders if given identical teams would generate very different results. The science part is the knowledge and skills of leadership that can be learned (e.g., defining clear business outcomes, strategic planning, commercial awareness). The art part is a mixture of psychology (the study of individual human behaviour), sociology (the study of groups of people) and how each unique leader applies the art and science to the challenge at hand. This book focuses primarily on the art of leadership, i.e., not so much *what* you do, but *how* you do it. Organisational culture is often referred to more simply as 'how things get done around here'. Companies with healthy cultures are 1.5 times more likely to experience revenue growth of 15% or more over three years.[1]

We all see examples of people who have the title of leader, but who currently have few willing followers. Let's be honest, it's unlikely they've picked up this book, or have a secure career ahead of them. If someone has gifted you this book it is because they see an even better leader in you and want to offer some guidance. Your initial reaction might be one of feeling judged, take a deep breath and allow the feeling to pass. Strong leadership requires both humility and confidence.

Ultimately, the process of leadership can be summarised in just three words:

Direction

Inspiration

Influence

Three words that are simple to say, but not easy to do. In fact, leading well is fiendishly difficult. What worked well just thirty years ago (before the world wide web) doesn't work in the knowledge age. What works well in a social care setting is unlikely to cut it in financial services. The devil is not so much in the detail, as in the context in which you're working.

There are so many leadership books, you could just roll your eyes and say there's nothing new under the sun. Certainly, knowledge about leadership isn't in short supply. What is in short supply are real world examples of how to apply leadership practices to the current context. In particular, examples that illustrate the tricky work of leading cultural transformation to enhance business outcomes.

Who Are The Authors?

It has been my privilege to collaborate with fellow leadership professionals to bring you a carefully curated selection of articles to save you re-inventing the wheel, making the same mistakes, or having to read gigabytes worth of ebooks. Our articles are informed by decades of developing leaders in progressive firms internationally, our individual experience of leading others, and reading voraciously on leadership.

Many of us are executive coaches too, so we've included provocative questions that meet you where you are and implore you to discover your difference that will make the difference. I already mentioned that context is critical, for that reason the authors selected for this book are familiar with the industry, objectives and pressures of our intended readers, but as you'd expect, they have a wide variety of experience, opinions and personalities.

We all come together through MPI Learning, (mpilearning.com), a business learning and development provider.

MPI Learning is committed to improving the world of work by supporting individuals and organisations to maximise their performance and impact on society. We create learning experiences and environments that provide you and your people with the workplace tools needed to succeed in today's ever-changing marketplace. Working with us will help you embed lifelong learning as a core part of your culture.

Who Is This Book For?

Our intended readers are those who are personally in a leadership position (or aspiring to be) and those who seek to nurture and develop leadership talent. In particular, it's for people who sense the need for a shift in 'how things get done around here' to enhance business outcomes, even if you can't define what that shift needs to be exactly. It's for pragmatic people who want actionable insights on how to break down culture transformation into tangible parts and understand the role of a leader in delivering change without damaging yourself, your people or your business results in the process.

The examples we provide are from a for-profit professional services context[2] i.e., you achieve business outcomes through people. We went with 'international' rather than global on the cover, because our thinking has a Western mindset bias, not because it's necessarily the best, but because it's what we know and where we operate.

It is our hope that this book will enable you to perform at your best, secure a long career and make a bigger difference.

Leadership Styles Change Over Time, Stay Informed, Stay Relevant

We believe that the fundamental process of leadership is timeless (direction, inspiration, influence), but the way in which we deliver the process is currently evolving every decade or so. Table 1 provides a simplified history of how context has changed leadership thinking.

(Period) Leadership Theory	Focus On...	Broader Context
(1940-1960) Behavioural	... the skills and actions of leaders	World War II Mass production Baby Boom
(1960-1990) Situational	...leaders adapting their style to their employees	The Digital Age
(1990-2000) Transactional or Transformational	... cost-benefit exchange of leaders/followers ... inspiring followers to higher performance	World Wide Web Dot Com Bubble European Union (Euro)
(2000+) Collaborative and Collective	... engaging followers by being person-centred ... the whole system of an organisation	September 11 Attacks Facebook and YouTube EU Expands to 25 countries Global Financial Crisis Covid-19 pandemic

Table 1: An overview of leadership styles and the context that informed them

Individuals and firms who are better adapted to the prevailing context will have a competitive advantage over those who are not as well adapted. Dive in to the chapters that follow to orientate yourself to the current context and how to evolve your leadership style to remain effective.

What's The Current Leadership Style?

In short, rapid advances in technology have accelerated the pace of change, driven a demand for greater transparency and made it possible to have relationships with anyone anywhere with the aid of a smartphone. As a result, the prevailing leadership styles are collaborative and collective (we need both) i.e., working across organisations to achieve a greater good.

Collaborative. Very few organisations can respond to changing market demands fast enough when compared to networks of specialist organisations working in partnership. Therefore, we need a collaborative leadership style that engages people across internal silos, across geography, and through partnerships with complementary suppliers.

Collective. These days we're only a few clicks away from live footage of events happening around the world and this creates a sense of a global community. Consider: the raised awareness of racial inequity following the murder of George Floyd, the ongoing war in Ukraine, the health and financial burden of the Covid-19 pandemic and, the increase in severe weather events. Such events, combined with conscious consumer buying power (e.g., eco-friendly products) ensure that corporate social responsibility (CSR) remains a priority. More than a priority, many organisations have made an aspect of CSR their core purpose aligned with the 17 UN Sustainable Development Goals[3].

What Do The Changes Mean For Me Personally, As A Leader?

Here are some examples of how the changes in technology, transparency and globalisation have required leaders to adapt how they direct, inspire and influence others, to collaborate in service of something greater than themselves.

Direction: Rapid advances in technology have accelerated the pace of change and this has changed how far ahead leaders can anticipate the future.

The speed of technology-led change is already faster than humans can evolve which demands that we play to our unique human strengths (e.g., creativity and compassion) and form collaborative partnerships with other specialist companies to remain nimble. Just recently, the need for social distancing during the Covid-19 pandemic accelerated the technology-adoption timeline for companies by seven years. That would have made a dent in your ten-year strategy! Realistically, setting the strategic direction for the next three years is now a reasonable planning horizon.

Inspiration: The demand for transparency requires leaders to be visible, personable and, role-models with integrity, and to not hide behind the role.

The desire for transparency has been driven in large part due to a ubiquitous social media presence, massive global interconnectivity and a platform for anyone to be an amateur broadcaster. The informal communication 'grapevine', once confined to interpersonal chit chat, now has the ability to go viral. A misstep that might once have gone under the radar is now played out publicly with potentially serious consequences for you personally, and the company brand. Salary information, once kept closely guarded, is now shared openly by individuals on employer review sites leading some employers to be completely transparent about pay scales. Ultimately, to inspire someone to a cause, would-be followers first need to know that you care, respect them and can be trusted. Integrity matters. So, say what you'll do, and do what you say.

Influence: Globalisation and our greater awareness of others requires leaders to act systemically within their company, and to understand how they can influence the wider systems in which they operate.

We are more technologically connected than we've ever been, we are therefore exposed to different thinking and ways of being than might be present in our usual social settings. In fact, we have access to the thoughts and opinions of people we'd never gain access to through hierarchy, social class or other societal constructs. Ultimately technological connectivity is doing a great job of holding leaders accountable for their actions on whole systems (e.g., climate, social justice). Technology also provides the platform to influence, and be influenced by, people far more widely than our own back yard. With great influence, comes great responsibility.

Change is ever present. Vigilance, perseverance, learning, and adaptability are crucial to ensuring ongoing success and long-term viability of your leadership and the firm you lead, hence our desire to create this book to support and challenge you as you navigate the 'new normal'.

A Word On Pronouns

We use a mixture of 'he', 'she' or 'they' when talking about leaders, in our view your gender identity has no bearing on your ability to demonstrate great leadership.

A Note From The Authors

We hope that by sharing our stories and expertise relevant to the current context you will take a moment to consider whether your leadership practices need tweaking.

- How has your business context changed in the last three years? How did you respond?

- In your own words, describe your firm's purpose, vision and the strategic direction.

- What do you do that inspires others? How do you know? Who inspires you?

- Who else do you need to influence to scale up your impact? Take a first step.

Further, we hope you will commit to applying the insights in the following chapters to strengthen your leadership and intentionally lead cultural transformation so that employees thrive, and the services of your firm remain valuable and vital to drive business outcomes.

Which Chapter Will Move You Forward Fastest?

We know demands are high and time is precious, so each chapter can be read in isolation, or read the book cover to cover, it's up to you.

Here's an overview of the chapters so you can see what will add most value to you today

Chapter 1 Welcome

Setting the scene to inspire curiosity about how the current context has informed the way we need to lead to remain relevant and commercially effective.

Leading the System

Chapter 2 Profit On Purpose (Angela Armstrong PhD)

Be intentional about your company culture by embedding a compelling purpose and a set of values-led behaviours. Business statistics show: doing good also means doing well commercially.

Chapter 3 Talent Liberation: How To Rethink Your Talent Strategy (Maggi Evans PhD)

How to find and liberate more of the talent that is currently lying dormant in your organisation.

Chapter 4 The Leaders' Role In Cultural Transformation (Angela Armstrong PhD)

Company culture, or 'how things get done around here', can be a competitive advantage that's hard to recreate, or it can undermine and slow efforts to progress. Discover the three golden rules for a successful transformation.

Leading Others to Achieve Business Outcomes

Chapter 5 Making The Complicated Happen (James Hall)

Achieve complex projects through people, by using clear and concise outcome-led instructions to unleash initiative and drive accountability.

Chapter 6 Psychological Safety – It's Real And It's Really Important (Nick Corbo)

Psychological safety is a critical factor in creating high performing teams. In addition to contributing diverse ideas and opinions, people can expect to have their ideas and thinking challenged in the spirit of achieving the best result. Without psychological safety, flawed thinking can end up driving strategy.

Chapter 7 Leading Small Teams (James Hall)

The opportunity to develop the leadership skills required to build a high-performing team is a great training ground for a future CEO.

Chapter 8 Five Steps To Leading A Stickier Business (Andy Goram)

Simple steps to create a place where people love to work, where they thrive, stay and attract more great talent to you.

Chapter 9 Inclusive Leadership: Look Through A Different Lens (Ellen Burton)

How you can positively impact your team and organization by practicing the skills and awareness essential to becoming an inclusive leader.

Leading Yourself

Chapter 10 Turning Self-Doubts To Self-Beliefs (Vanessa Boon)

Learn self-belief techniques for you, and the team you are nurturing. Free people from the doubts that hold them back to unlock untapped potential for business success.

Chapter 11 Influencing Without Authority (Susan Croft)

Discover the six skills that affect your power to influence without authority, so that you can collaborate to achieve aspirational business outcomes far beyond the capacity and capability of your direct reports.

Chapter 12 How To Enable Empathetic Leadership (Matthew Storey)

Empathy, a core skill of leadership, is taking on a new level of meaning and priority because people are experiencing multiple kinds of stress. Demonstrating empathy is positive for people, and new research demonstrates its importance for everything from innovation to retention.

Chapter 13 How Not To Be An Inclusive Leader (Vanessa Boon)

Learn the mistakes and pitfalls to avoid, plus adventures in self-discovery, tongue-in-cheek pointers and the collective learning from facilitating courageous conversations with thousands of people on this topic

Chapter 14 How To Become A Trusted Leader (Fraser Murray)

Trust is ultimately a character-based phenomenon, we trust people's judgment in the 'moments that matter'. The ability to develop and adapt your character strengths can differentiate you as a leader with strong values, who acts with integrity to trim costs, grow profits and create innovative solutions.

Chapter 15 Next Steps

Partnering with MPI Learning is a bold and vital decision to deliver the organisational culture that differentiates your company and provides an unassailable competitive advantage. If you want to find out more, we'd love to talk to you, please get in touch.

You can start anywhere in this book but dip into this book often. The authors are all high achieving professionals who are at the very forefront of leadership development, internationally.

Start now. It will be time well-spent.

References

1. https://www.achievers.com/blog/organizational-culture-definition/ [accessed 29 Oct 2022]

2. (employees with a high knowledge base providing specialist or specific services)

3. https://sdgs.un.org/goals [accessed 28 October 2022]

About Angela Armstrong PhD

Angela Armstrong PhD is a master coach, learning professional, and author.

Born and educated in the UK, Angela has repeatedly achieved top level performance academically (MBA, PhD, CIPD), professionally (top 5% performance at Accenture, non-executive director), commercially (business owner for ten years) and as a thought-leader (author of best-selling book *The Resilience Club*).

Angela inspires leaders and subject matter experts across Europe and the US to expand their self-awareness, assess the systemic context in which they work, and discover their authentic leadership style. So that they can better anticipate the shifting needs, priorities and approaches of their industry, clients and employees to deliver business outcomes, profitably and purposefully.

Angela has led, managed, and facilitated organisational culture change for over two decades. Her capability and candour inspire cultural shift by embracing sceptics during discussions, informing intention into action and emboldening people to find their voice.

Personal interests include outdoor pursuits, grassroots travel (50+ countries), soulful connections, spirited adventures and creative expression.

Linkedin *https://www.linkedin.com/in/angelakarmstrong/*

MPI Learning *www.mpilearning.com*

Leading the System

Profit On Purpose

Angela Armstrong PhD

Promise

Business outcomes show that doing good (for people and planet) also means doing well commercially (profit). So, be intentional about your company culture by embedding a compelling purpose and a set of values-led behaviours.

Key Messages

- The context shift from profit *or* purpose, to profit *on* purpose

- The value of purpose: gives employees a meaningful reason to collaborate, enhances corporate reputation, and is a fundamental part of business ethics.

- The purpose of values: a set of values-led behaviours guide how employees think, act, and communicate as an expression of your brand.

Prior to about 2000 most commercial organisations posted their vision (what our company's future looks like) and mission statements (how we propose to achieve the vision) in company reports and on posters around their offices. The purpose of the organisation was deemed obvious: to generate profit, by legal means, so that shareholders continued to invest in the company.

A noble purpose statement espousing collective effort for a greater societal good has long been the norm for charitable organisations. For example, Oxfam International 'Together, we fight inequality to end poverty and injustice.'

What shifted? People's conscious awareness of their ability to impact on climate and social justice through their daily choices, basically consumer demand and employee expectations. The 2007-8 financial crisis followed a string of financial scandals including the collapse of Enron in 2001 and Lehman Brothers in 2008. These scandals put the spotlight on poor behaviours in the pursuit of profit and consumers shifted their focus towards organisations with more ethical business practices. In addition, recent changes in technology, transparency, globalisation, and medical advances have resulted in a multi-generational and highly mobile workforce with no expectation of a 'job for life'. Time is our most precious commodity and people want more than a salary; they want to collaborate in service of something greater than themselves, to make a difference. Shareholders want leaders to adapt quickly to maximise profits. Shareholders, employees, and consumers are vital for commerce, so leaders have had to adapt to the new context, or risk becoming redundant. Of course, many C-suite leaders have embraced profit on purpose with great passion.

A meaningful purpose incorporates three core elements – why the organisation exists and what it stands for; the impact of the business on the environment and people – employees, the communities we interact with and society.

Here's an example from Visa (payment services).

Unlocking opportunities for everyone

We're a trusted network and world leader in digital payments, with a mission to remove barriers and connect more people to the global economy. Because we believe that economies that include everyone, everywhere uplift everyone, everywhere. (Visa, 2022)[1]

What Is The Value Of Purpose?

A purpose expresses an organisation's reason for existing, commitment to its community and environment and demonstrates its core identity. Successfully articulated and embedded, a purpose unites stakeholders behind the organisation, enhances corporate reputation and ensures that employees feel they are part of a wider socially valued endeavour. It is also a fundamental component of business ethics.

Some of the firms recognised in 2022 by Ethisphere on their annual 'World's Most Ethical Company' list[2] include: Accenture (consultancy), Aflac Incorporated (insurance), IBM (IT services), Infosys (software and services), Mastercard (payment services), Microsoft (technology), Nokia (telecom), Old National Bank (bank), Pfizer (pharmaceuticals), Prudential (financial services), Visa (payment services), Workday (software and services).

It turns out that doing good, also means doing well commercially.

'A Harvard Business Review study found that when companies had clarity of purpose which was widely understood in the organization, they had better growth as compared with companies which hadn't developed or leveraged their purpose. Specifically, 52% of purpose-driven companies experienced over 10% growth compared with

42% of non-purpose-driven companies. Purpose-driven companies benefitted from greater global expansion (66% compared with 48%), more product launches (56% compared with 33%) and success in major transformation efforts (52% compared with 16%)'[3]

What Is Your Company Purpose?

The question is not should your business have a purpose, but does it have a purpose that is meaningful and that everyone knows and understands? A purpose cannot be developed in isolation. Involve the whole leadership team and incorporate input from all parts of the business and with input from employees at every level. The quality of the conversation will be richer, and more engaging as a result. Don't rush this step, give the conversations time and space, so that ideas can marinade and be revisited before settling on the final wording.

'Your purpose needs to be both aspirational and practical. It is meant to give employees a compelling and meaningful reason to collaborate, and convey to employees who they must be together to add the greatest value AND about what should be on their meeting agendas?' If it doesn't do both, your purpose isn't fulfilling its role or value.'[4]

What Is The Purpose Of Values?

One of the many benefits of being purpose-driven, is that it has a unifying effect on both internal and external stakeholders.

Determining organisational values changes the way people in the organisation think, act, and communicate and has a positive impact on how the business operates.

Purpose drives values, and values drive behaviour.

Defining Your Company Values

Your company values express the beliefs, philosophies, and principles that support your purpose. Values shape your organisational culture, impact your business strategy and improve team cohesion. Some commonly declared values include integrity, passion, fairness, diversity, and inclusion.

It might be tempting to develop a long list of values, but a short list is easier to communicate and for employees to remember, connect with, and consistently practice. Prioritise three to five values for maximum effectiveness.

Some questions to help you define your company values:

- What values support our purpose?

- What must we do as table stakes? (e.g. regulatory and compliance frameworks)

- What do we need to care about to be a success?

- What separates us from our competitors?

- The principles of what is regarded as right and wrong in the organisation?

- How do we act and behave in certain and different situations?

- What aspects of our character are we most proud of?

- What are our non-negotiables when it comes to interpersonal behaviour?

- How would internal and external stakeholders describe your values?

- What are the motives behind the purpose?

Three Tips From Years Of Facilitating Value Discovery Workshops

1. Start with the behaviour, not the value label – it's seductive to land on a label for your value first e.g. 'We are always innovative ……'.- hurrah! Ask your teams to share how they create new ideas with each other and for their customers – what do they do currently? What does that look like and sound like? How would your customers describe the impact on them?

2. Use an external and internal lens to describe your value-driven behaviour. Describe how your customers would experience this value as well as internal colleagues.

3. We suggest 80% of your values should reflect your current DNA, that is, reflect the behaviours (magic dust) that people experience and have always experienced. It can also be helpful to have 20% aspirational values – what behaviours are going to be important for you to reach your purpose in the future?

Ensuring Values Generate Consistent Desired Behaviours

Values are worthless unless they drive consistent behaviours. During the 2007-8 financial crisis, how many institutions involved in the scandals had *Integrity* listed on their values poster? Do you consider the behaviour of these organisations to have been congruent with their stated value?

Defining your values *with* your employees, rather than *for* them is a great opportunity to engage hearts and minds, and ultimately ensure that the values selected are understood at a practical level in terms of the behaviours they drive. Defining your company values involves discussions that inevitably touch on our personal values. The conversation might feel unfamiliar, we rarely try to evaluate and articulate how we collaborate, but it's time well spent.

Another reason I am personally passionate about values is that, well-defined, they provide the underpinning for a diverse and inclusive workforce. Every organisation serves a community comprised of people from all sorts of backgrounds, ethnicities, ages and so on. However, if the recruitment and selection phases seek to hire for 'does the face fit', interview panels often discount the value of people who are less like themselves. Instead, hiring for a 'values fit' gives permission for a wider expression of behaviours that still deliver on the underlying value.

As a simple example the value of integrity necessitates that people speak up when they notice something they think is amiss. Some people might call it out vocally and in public, others might prefer to maintain anonymity and relay the information to a third party they trust rather than offer a direct challenge – does it matter as long as the incongruity is brought to the attention of someone with the ability to act on the information?

Three further ways to embed your purpose and values in the company culture

1. **Communicate, Communicate, Communicate.** Your purpose will drive your strategic objectives (the what) and your values will provide the behaviours (the how). Seek opportunities for dialogue to engage and embed your purpose and values from town hall events to one-to-one line manager conversations.

2. **Role-model the behaviours.** People always look up, your employees are more likely to believe and behave congruently with your values if they see their leaders and managers role-modelling the desired behaviours consistently.

3. **Consistently and congruently weave them into all facets of company culture** from office décor to policies, organisational

chart to promotion criteria and beyond. This topic is covered more fully in the chapter 'The leaders' role in culture transformation'.

Developing your purpose and value-driven behaviour with your employees, and embedding it daily is, and will continue to be, an essential leadership capability. An inspiring purpose is powerful, the time and energy you invest in this will reap rewards. So, be patient, be open, listen deeply and let your inspiring purpose and values evolve from the best that every contributor has to offer.

References

1. www.visa.com

2. https://worldsmostethicalcompanies.com/honorees/ [accessed 1 November 2022]

3. https://www.forbes.com/sites/tracybrower/2021/08/22/the-power-of-purpose-and-why-it-matters-now/?sh=1b4db369163a [accessed 1 Nov 2022]

4. Valdes-Dapena, C. (2008). Lessons from Mars, John Hunt Publishing.

About Angela Armstrong PhD

Angela Armstrong PhD is a master coach, learning professional, and author.

Born and educated in the UK, Angela has repeatedly achieved top level performance academically (MBA, PhD, CIPD), professionally (top 5% performance at Accenture, non-executive director), commercially (business owner for ten years) and as a thought-leader (author of best-selling book *The Resilience Club*).

Angela inspires leaders and subject matter experts across Europe and the US to expand their self-awareness, assess the systemic context in which they work, and discover their authentic leadership style. So that they can better anticipate the shifting needs, priorities and approaches of their industry, clients and employees to deliver business outcomes, profitably and purposefully.

Angela has led, managed, and facilitated organisational culture change for over two decades. Her capability and candour inspire cultural shift by embracing sceptics during discussions, informing intention into action and emboldening people to find their voice.

Personal interests include outdoor pursuits, grassroots travel (50+ countries), soulful connections, spirited adventures and creative expression.

Linkedin *https://www.linkedin.com/in/angelakarmstrong/*

MPI Learning *www.mpilearning com*

Talent Liberation:
How To Rethink Your Talent Strategy

Maggi Evans PhD

Promise

This chapter will help you to liberate more of the talent that is currently lying dormant in your organisation.

Key Messages

- There is no shortage of talent – we need to think ahead, to look in new places so we can find and untap the talent we need.

- Talent is about more than individual talent heroes – it's also about a culture that enables teams and individuals to perform at their best.

- Each talent strategy is unique – it should be based on a deep understanding of the risks and opportunities for our business (not simply adopting processes done by everyone else).

Have you ever looked around you and worried about the lack of talent moving through your organisation? If so, you are not alone. Leaders often tell me that lack of the 'right' people is one of the biggest limitations to the growth and success of their business. They describe feeling disempowered, that unless they are paying the top salaries or have a fantastic brand reputation, they are not going to be attractive to the 'best' people, so they are destined to lose out in the so called 'war for talent'. Despite several decades of investment in talent strategy, high potential programmes, succession planning and nine box grids etc, leaders are still worried about the availability of talent.

So, what is going wrong, why hasn't talent management delivered?

I love a complex puzzle, so a few years ago, I set out to understand why current talent strategies weren't delivering the promised transformation, and, what could be done instead. My research involved interviews with industry leaders, conversations with 'talented' people, case studies, academic articles, prototyping fresh approaches (and a PhD and book along the way).[1]

It was fascinating. One of the first things I found was that most talent strategies are based on three assumptions that inform all the action. The first assumption is that talent is scarce – there isn't enough of it, so we have to 'fight' to get our share.

Secondly, there is a focus on individual talent heroes, who are seen to hold the key to unlocking organisational success.

Thirdly, there is an emphasis on putting in the right processes to track, map and act. However, when you look beneath the surface, these assumptions don't survive much scrutiny. Indeed, many of the approaches were developed in the 1950s for a world that was far more stable and predictable than the one we find ourselves in (a time when a five-year succession plan and a ten-year business strategy was actually likely to go unchanged!).

Talent liberation challenges these three assumptions and offers a fresh approach to workforce and talent planning at organisational, functional and departmental level. It reframes the approach to talent, moving from trying to manage and control it, to finding ways to harness and set it free. In many ways it echoes the changes introduced in software development by the 'agile' movement[2] (but unlike the agile movement, talent liberation was not developed on a ski trip to Utah!). In doing this, I have built on the work of other writers (such as Jeffery Pfeffer, Malcolm Gladwell, Rob Briner, Bob Sutton, Amy Edmondson, Paul Sparrow and David Collings). The intention of Talent Liberation is to point to a new blueprint for a flexible and holistic talent approach and right now, this is just what we need.

There Is No Shortage Of Talent

Within talent conversations, it's easy to adopt a 'mindset of scarcity', assuming that there just isn't enough talent to go round because it's a finite resource. It's true, there might be huge challenges in the availability of talented people who are visible to us as 'ready now' and who fulfil all the criteria on our wish list. However, that does not mean that we have a shortage of talented people who can be 'ready in the future'.

As an example, in 1865, Elizabeth Garett Anderson became the first qualified woman doctor in the UK (over 300 years after the College of Physicians first introduced licensing for Doctors). By 1911, there were 495 women on the medical register and now, within the 30-34 age group, 57% of doctors identify as female. This is surely a reflection of increased social and educational opportunity to develop valuable skills, rather than a change in the underlying potential or 'talent' of women. Applied to the workplace, this example can help us to see the opportunity to look beyond the people who are 'ready now' and to consider how much talent is around us that is lying dormant, waiting to be harnessed and developed. If we can identify and develop these people, there is no need for a shortage in talent.

One leader I spoke to recently described having access to a 'talent puddle instead of a talent pool'. If that is the situation you find yourself in, you might find these questions helpful:

- How much visibility do you have of people's skills, motivations and commitment?

- Do you really know what your people are capable of, or do you make assumptions based on what they are doing now?

- How do you encourage and support the potential of people who might tend to be 'hidden' talent, for example, people from under-represented groups?

- What groups of people might have parallel skills or experiences who you could quickly develop?

- Are you still wedded to traditional views of how you employ people, or have you broadened your talent pools to include ways to borrow, redeploy, reskill or share talent?

- How can you leverage the opportunities of remote working to access new sources of talent?

- How can technology enable different ways of working and different requirements?

Exploring these questions can lead to very different conversations and solutions to any lack of 'ready now' talent. For example, there are organisations who have championed social diversity and accessed significant new talent, businesses who have introduced flexible contracts designed specifically to appeal to returning retirees, and companies who now access global talent as they have removed their requirement for people to be in the office three days per week. What could you do?

Talent Is About More Than Individual Talent Heroes

Many organisations I work with become obsessed by their 'high potential' talent, focusing the majority of their talent effort on attracting, selecting, developing and retaining this group. The assumption is that 'talent' is a trait that some people possess, and if you put a talented person or leader in place, success will naturally follow. Unfortunately, it does not seem that simple, and we will all know examples of highly successful leaders or sports people who were not able to repeat their success in a different environment. This suggests that there are other things at play too, and if we want to drive organisational success, we should look beyond individual talent at other enablers of success. My research indicated the importance of balancing an individual talent focus with developing a culture that values team effort and that enables every individual to perform at their best.

The importance of teams is often overlooked in traditional talent strategies. This is despite research showing that effective teams often out-perform collections of talented individuals (something that can also be seen on sports fields around the world). Moreover, many predictions about the future of work indicate that organisations with strong collaboration, agile teams and openness to change will have a competitive advantage, and one that is built into their DNA and therefore hard for competitors to replicate.

- If talented teams are an essential part of your future success, what are you doing to support the growth of teams?
- How do you accelerate their performance?
- How do you encourage and reward team collaboration and success?
- How can you incorporate a team lens into your talent strategy?

Some of the organisations work with have developed 'new team formation' programmes that accelerate the performance of new teams through a 30-day plan including visioning success, collaborative target setting, ways or working, team relationship and trust building. Such activities are then regularly followed up within the talent processes.

The other key point that emerged from my research was the opportunity to invest in actions to increase everyone's performance, not just focus on the high potentials. According to 2022 data from Gallup[3], 19% of workers are actively disengaged, and only 21% describe themselves as thriving at work. Not surprisingly, thriving and positive engagement are associated with greater discretionary effort and higher performance of the individual and the organisation. This surely merits being part of a talent strategy, taking a more inclusive approach to increase the performance of the many, not just the few. If you think you can unlock more talent across your organisation, you could start by asking people the powerful question suggested by Aaron Dignan[4], 'what's stopping you from doing the best work of your life?'.

Leaders and managers who ask this question (and act on what they hear) have unlocked talent in many ways, for example, greater empowerment, improved processes leading to reduced re-work, better cross function collaboration and greater manager feedback.

Each Talent Strategy Is Unique

Many organisations have typically taken a 'plug and play' approach to talent, adopting approaches such as succession planning and nine box grids because that's what other organisations do. These approaches can take huge amounts of effort, with HR teams spending months pulling data and presentations together for an annual 'talent review'. But all this effort doesn't seem to be bringing returns, and most leaders describe their talent processes as adding little value. This was beautifully summed up by one of my clients who told me, 'We've got so wrapped up in the process of talent management, we've forgotten what its purpose is'. In essence, the purpose of a talent strategy is to minimise risk and to maximise opportunities for competitive advantage. The nature of these risks and opportunities will be fundamentally different for each organisation, depending on the environment, strategy, business model and the possible scenarios that the organisation faces. For example, the overall purpose may be responsiveness to changing client needs, being able to quickly scale parts of the business up or down. For another organisation, the purpose might be lowest cost of delivery or retention of unique knowledge. Whatever it is, the clarity of purpose needs to be central to the rest of the talent and workforce plan.

Once the purpose is clear, there can be an overhaul of talent processes. The only processes to survive should be those that genuinely make a contribution. Alongside this, new processes may be needed. For example, based on such an overhaul, some clients focus their effort on increasing talent visibility, others on broadening their ecosystem, or sharing and deploying talent in more flexible ways. Other organisations empower individuals to develop the skills needed for the future, telling them about the new 'in demand' skills and supporting them to develop themselves. There are numerous solutions, but they need to be based on solving your problem, on understanding and minimising the risks of your business and maximising the opportunities. These talent processes may look and feel different to previous processes, they may be owned by managers and individuals rather than HR, they might be promoted rather than enforced... there should be no assumptions in the best way to drive the talent strategy that you need.

There are huge business opportunities to unlock by rethinking your talent strategy. Liberating more of the talent that is lying dormant can be transformative, and it can be done across the whole organisation, or within your part of it. The first step is to reflect, to challenge your assumptions about talent, to get under the skin of what is going on in your business, and what you need for the future. Through reviewing data and through conversations with leaders, HR and team members, you can build a picture of the risks and opportunities in your business. You can then focus your efforts on solving your own talent puzzle.

References

1. Evans, M., Arnold, J. and Rothwell, A., 2019. From Talent Management to Talent Liberation: A Practical Guide for Professionals, Managers and Leaders. Routledge.

2. See History: The Agile Manifesto accessed 19.10.22

3. State of the Global Workplace Report - Gallup accessed 19.10.22

4. Dignan, Aaron. Brave new work: Are you ready to reinvent your organization?. Penguin, 2019.

About Maggi Evans PhD

Maggi Evans PhD is an experienced consultant with international experience across a variety of sectors including banking, professional services, FMCG, technology and retail. Recognised as an influential communicator, Maggi combines challenging strategic thinking with realistic and  practical solutions. She has a reputation as an insightful consultant, helping clients to gain new perspectives and to reduce the 'noise' around a challenge so they can focus and act on key issues which will make a difference.

Her specific areas of interest and expertise include people strategy, top team (assessment, coaching and team development), leadership development and culture change. She is on a mission to help organisations, leaders and individuals to liberate talent through creating organisations where everyone can thrive and do their best work. She regularly speaks at conferences on talent strategy and is the author of an award winning book on talent management.

LinkedIn *www.linkedin.com/in/maggievans*

MPI Learning *www.mpilearning com*

The Leaders' Role In Culture Transformation

Angela Armstrong PhD

Promise

Prioritise these three aspects of change to avoid overwhelm and deliver what really matters in cultural transformation without breaking yourself, your people or the business in the process.

Key Messages

* Influence – Organisational culture is a self-sustaining system, to effect behaviour change, leaders must role model the desired behaviours and evolve the environment **coherently.**

* Inspiration – Actions speak louder than words, but words matter a great deal too. People buy people, so leaders need to be personable, visible and **consistent** to move people from good intentions to profitable outcomes.

* Direction – Set a realistic **pace** of change, so that there are more winners than losers at every step, to minimise resistance and create self-sustaining change.

What's So Important About Culture Anyway?

Company culture, or 'How things get done around here', can be a competitive advantage that's hard to recreate, or it can undermine and slow efforts to progress.

Company culture has far-reaching implications for what work gets prioritised, how much gets done, the way in which it is done, whether employees contribute their best talents, how the brand of the company is perceived, and of course business outcomes. Basically, it's vital to the long-term success of your business and can be valued as an intangible asset when selling a company.

Being intentional about company culture (see the chapter Profit on Purpose for definition of purpose and values) has been empirically proven to stabilize organisations and help them succeed. Of course, shaping company culture happens every day, through every interaction, whether it's intentional or not.

It Takes Forever To Change Culture, Doesn't It?

Not necessarily. Savvy social media influencers are exhibiting leadership practices and affecting cultural change – directing like-minded followers to protest, inspiring people to find their voice, influencing policy and process change. Examples include *#metoo #blacklivesmatter*. Of course, effective leadership is also practised by those with a very different agenda to our own, some of whom might be in your organisation, at any level.

Isn't It Hard To Change Organisational Culture?

Yes, if you're not doing it right! I've been leading, facilitating and consulting on large-scale culture transformation for two decades, sometimes from the initial concept, other times stepping in to troubleshoot failing programmes. If things go awry, it's always the same three root causes, and the senior leadership team always carry the can.

Ultimately the job of the leader in any transformation is 'to make it make sense'.

Take care of these three root causes of cultural change failure and the rest will resolve as a consequence, *Oh look, they map to the processes of leadership: direction, inspiration and influence. Who knew?*

Let's start with Influence...

Influence – Our Experience Of The External Environment Influences Our Behaviour

In order to influence someone, you first need to know what already influences them. Typically, thoughts turn immediately to what engages people, what is perhaps less obvious is the huge influence our experience of the environment around us has on our behaviour. I'm not only referring to our physical environment here, it's also the policies, organisational structures and colleague behaviours etc. Taken together these practical, tangible artefacts are the 'way things get done around here', that is, the organisational culture. If we want behaviour change to stick, we also have to change the environment in which it is practised.

Organisational culture is a self-sustaining system, if you want to transform it you have to act on the entire system simultaneously (see Figure 1) or else the other components pull it back to the status quo. This means you need to co-ordinate your change champions in different areas of the business (HR, Legal, Operations etc). Organisational culture reveals itself in every experience someone has of your company, and it is absorbed (often subconsciously) even by ad-hoc visitors, so imagine the daily impact on your employees.

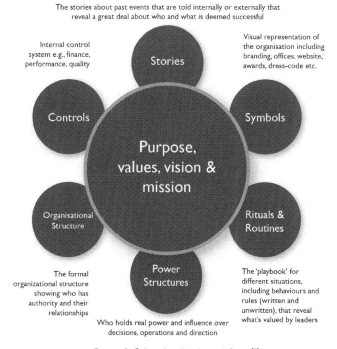

Figure 1 Cultural web adapted from [1]

Key culture assets include a manifesto (purpose, mission, vision, values), organisation chart, role descriptions, on-boarding process, performance review process, learning and development programmes, employee remuneration and reward structure, standard operating procedures, communication tools, disciplinary and complaints policy and key performance indicators.

The culture assets provide clear guideposts that support new colleagues to integrate into the organisation and accelerate their speed to value. Also, these assets contribute to a company valuation, because organisational culture can be a competitive advantage and extraordinarily hard to replicate.

Culture assets are created for the whole employee lifecycle and need to be congruent and consistent when viewed as a whole set. When different aspects of culture seem incongruent it gives mixed messages that cause uncertainty, questions about fairness, and reduced trust. As a ludicrously simple example, imagine you're running late for your train, you notice that the train cab shows one destination and the display on the platform indicates another, you hesitate, the doors close, you'll have to wait. The same is true of mixed messages during culture change, your job as a leader is to 'make it make sense' so that more people move forward without hesitation.

For example, (I've seen this one too often), if your internal communications promote employee wellbeing and bowls of fruit are made freely available, but long-hours are expected, the offices are open at the weekend and only workaholics are promoted then the environmental messages are not coherent. People will tend towards either wellbeing or work-focused, strike a balance between the two, or fluctuate between the extremes, and a range of experience stories will be told about your company. Whichever culture you were intending to promote will have lacklustre success at best... unless you 'make it make sense'.

Many organisations are working towards making EDI (equity, diversity and inclusion) a central part of their culture. The organisations doing this well are focusing internally first, getting their own house in order, raising awareness, consulting with employees, altering policies and practices that can be improved. Some companies went for a 'rebrand' option initially, changing website rhetoric and imagery, hiring non-exec directors from under-represented groups and making much of their supposed EDI credentials on social media. A focus on *being seen* to do EDI well, but not actually *delivering* EDI well, has often resulted in a cynical and resistant backlash that makes effective change more effortful.

Let's pick up on 'how' to influence as we turn to the leadership process of 'inspiration'.

Inspiration – Consistent Actions Speak Louder Than Words

Culture change is about getting people to conduct themselves in alignment with the purpose and values of the firm so that they represent an extension of the brand, whilst achieving business results. If you've ever embarked on a new fitness regime or otherwise tried to change your behaviour, you know the new behaviours are only sustainable when you *want* to do it, not when it feels like something you *should* do. Therefore, inspiring others to behave differently requires us to move hearts *and* minds. If you want others to be passionate about something, let them see you being passionate about it. The thing is, it needs to be authentic to be believable.

- In your own words, articulate *why* the company purpose is *personally* important to you, tell the story of a genuine personal experience that demonstrates you 'get' the purpose and you're emotionally invested in achieving it.

- Take time to align (at least some of) your personal values with those of the organisation, or else why are you working here?

- Arrange a focus group with a cross section of people from the organisation to discuss what the company values would look like in terms of observable behaviours, communicate the outcomes. Then role model the behaviours that reflect the organisational values. For example, what does 'courage' look like?

Speaking up when you have a view that's different to the majority, taking a calculated risk etc.

When people can see it, they can be it. We're not after lots of mini-me replicas here, it is possible to exhibit aligned behaviours *and* allow our unique personality to shine.

To inspire effectively, role modelling requires consistency, which provides a sense of security and stability – people know what they're going to get from interactions with you. Whether that's in the meeting, in the corridor, walking across the car park, commenting on social media, anything that can be found in an internet search... you on a good day, you on a bad day – you get the idea.

We are more technologically connected than we've ever been, and often less interpersonally connected (e.g. a table of people in a cafe and each of them is looking at their smart phone). It is possible to connect at a human level using technology, it's just that often we allow the physical distance to also be an emotional one. Don't let remote-working become an excuse for poor relationship building.

During the pandemic, when social distancing forced a shift to far more remote working than had previously been the case, the leaders who were consistently themselves first and used technology as a tool to express their character second, found that the transition was significantly smoother. Rather than relish the lack of commuting for site visits, they found creative ways to attend with social distancing, or made arrangements to be 'carried around' by someone who was on site via on a mobile device to 'meet' the team and see progress.

The usual 'open door policy' on a Friday afternoon was replaced with an open Zoom call that anyone could join. Rather than a veneer of 'everything's fine' they shared their anecdotes of now having small or furry colleagues (children and pets) that were by turns amusing and challenging, just as they would have in the office kitchen. In short, they allowed themselves to be seen both personally and professionally, and it invited others to do the same. The blurring of boundaries didn't suit everyone, but I would wager that, for many, it forged better interpersonal relationships with colleagues than had previously been the case.

Leading cultural transformation demands all of you, not only *what* you do, but also *how* you conduct yourself whilst doing it. Everyone will be looking to you to set the example, so you have to be visible. To effect change, leaders have to go first, and alone, at least until others start to follow. You might feel exposed, vulnerable and uncertain. You might err and get called out, that's what happens when you're learning under a microscope. How you respond and make amends has value, it gives other people permission to try out the new behaviours and be imperfect whilst they learn. Role-modelling new behaviours consistently requires a good degree of emotional intelligence, self-discipline and self-confidence. If it was easy, everyone would do it.

The leadership team need to be role-modelling and upholding the organisational culture in lock step, visibly and consistently.

You'll likely have a whole communications team handling that side of things.

However, you can support them greatly by:

- reiterating the key messages even when you've said them so many times that you're saying them in your sleep.

- remaining open to questions, even if you have to get back to people with answers later.

- telling it as it is, no better, no worse; it's significantly more reassuring than relentless cheerleading.

Now we have an idea of what we're changing and how to move hearts and minds let's move to the final root cause that inhibits successful change programmes – Direction, and more particularly the pace at which it's possible to move in that direction.

Direction – A Considered Pace: Ensure There Are More Winners Than Losers At Every Step

Unless you have a highly experienced team of change managers estimating the change timeline I'd offer this general rule of thumb, take your first conservative estimate of how long you think the change will take, then double it. Revisit the expected timeline every quarter. Much like building a house it can seem to take forever to get the foundations in place and then the rest of the house gets built in no time at all.

Here are three disciplines to inform the pace of change, so that consistent progress is made at a speed the organisation has the capacity to absorb, without damaging yourself, your people, or business outcomes in the process. Whilst it may not seem quite as exciting, slow and steady progress initially means that lessons can be learned and applied on a manageable scale with minimum adverse impact. As confidence builds, and more people (18% of the impacted population) are integrating the changes as their new ways of working, the self-sustaining nature of organisational culture kicks in and accelerates the pace at which sustainable change can occur.

Consult: People don't resist change; they resist being changed. When creating or approving the cultural transformation timeline, ensure that sufficient time is allowed at the outset to consult and co-create solutions with representatives of impacted stakeholder groups. A genuinely consultative process is vital to the success of your transformation. As a minimum it will enable you to optimise timing (avoid disrupting the finance department at end-of-year). minimising the risk of overlooking something fundamental (like a whole stakeholder group, it happens!), create better informed solutions, and reduce resistance (because co-creating the solution means stakeholders are personally invested in the solution). Sounds obvious? All I'm going to say is that a fake consult that is actually persuading people to agree with some pre-conceived solution always backfires.

More winners than losers at every step: Whether you are creating or approving the cultural transformation timeline, apply the litmus test of 'more winners than losers at every step' to ensure that the business continues to function well during the transition period. As we've already seen organisational culture is a system of self-reinforcing elements that must all be acted on simultaneously. Therefore, it's unrealistic and impractical to try and change the cultural environment for the whole employee base at the same time. We also want to ensure that the informal communication grapevine is positive about the forthcoming changes, so it makes sense to have more people positively reacting to the change than naysayers at each stage of implementation. Having done a consult phase, it should be possible to identify sub-groups where they exist e.g., region, division, department, building, floor-plate, team. To assess whether the size of the impacted population in each step is achievable use the change formula, popularised by Dannemiller[2] which uses a mathematical expression to articulate the factors to consider.

Sustainable change is possible if $(D \times V \times F) > R$

D = dissatisfaction with the current state

V = vision of the future

F = size and clarity of first steps

R = anticipated resistance.

In other words, the dissatisfaction, vision and first steps for the impacted stakeholder group, when taken into consideration together, must be greater than the anticipated resistance from the impacted stakeholder group, and none of DVF can be missing. If it is judged that the resistance would be greater than DVF taken together then stop and find ways to improve D, V, or F. If that's not possible then lower the resistance by choosing a smaller impacted stakeholder group e.g., splitting the group into two phases of implementation.

If you only ever remember one thing about change management, make it this equation. If anything is not going to plan, the answer and the solution are in the equation.

Listen to the grapevine. The informal communication grapevine is faster than the speed of light; gain access, and listen! Of course, your comms team will have ensured that formal feedback mechanisms are in place so they can see how the official communications about the changes are received. A classic solution is the 'you said, we did' communications to show that feedback is being responded to. But often, the golden nuggets of information that tell you how well the transformation is going (or not), are only available via the informal grapevine, which in practical terms is often via a technology enabled instant messenger app on people's smartphones. It's unlikely that you, as the leader, will have been invited, so here's where your change champions and impacted stakeholder representatives can provide valuable insight on the grapevine themes back to the change leaders. Now, better informed decisions can be made about remedial action if necessary, or the pace of change altered.

Cultural leadership is especially important during the merging of two or more organisations, each with their own unique culture. Cultures that often clash in some aspects, leading to ego-driven conflict, communication problems and identity crisis. Rather than adopt one or the other culture it's up to leaders to facilitate the merger by revisiting the definition of culture with the new combined employee base.

This example of getting the pace completely wrong is from during the financial crisis. Two retail banks were forced by the

UK government to merge within several months, something that was only possible in the minds of politicians. You might get the data and technology consolidated by then, but consider the emotional change curve of the employees and customer bases of the two banks who had spent decades differentiating themselves from one another! In their haste the change team instructed the redecoration of the smaller bank in the bigger bank's branding, including all printed collateral, office building (inside and out), even the lanyards and ID tags of employees in the space of a weekend. People left the offices one colour on Friday and came back to a completely different visual of their workplace on Monday. Can you imagine? In fact, there was a communication leak somewhere and the employee grapevine had gone into overdrive. Looking across the floorplate on Monday it was evident that every employee originally from the smaller bank was wearing their old 'team colours'. The gross insensitivity of the unannounced rebranding of head office, a dominant building on the high street, in a city where the bank was one of the main employers, was a public humiliation whose scars live on in the stories that are still told over a decade later.

References

1.   Figure 1: 'Fundamentals of Strategy' by G. Johnson, R. Whittington, and K. Scholes. Published by Pearson Education, 2012.

2.   Dannemiller, K. D., & Jacobs, R. W. (1992). Changing the way organizations change: A revolution of common sense. The Journal of Applied Behavioral Science, 28(4), 480–498.

About Angela Armstrong PhD

Angela Armstrong PhD is a master coach, learning professional, and author.

Born and educated in the UK, Angela has repeatedly achieved top level performance academically (MBA, PhD, CIPD), professionally (top 5% performance at Accenture, non-executive director), commercially (business owner for ten years) and as a thought-leader (author of best-selling book *The Resilience Club*).

Angela inspires leaders and subject matter experts across Europe and the US to expand their self-awareness, assess the systemic context in which they work, and discover their authentic leadership style. So that they can better anticipate the shifting needs, priorities and approaches of their industry, clients and employees to deliver business outcomes, profitably and purposefully.

Angela has led, managed, and facilitated organisational culture change for over two decades. Her capability and candour inspire cultural shift by embracing sceptics during discussions, informing intention into action and emboldening people to find their voice.

Personal interests include outdoor pursuits, grassroots travel (50+ countries), soulful connections, spirited adventures and creative expression.

Linkedin https://www.linkedin.com/in/angelakarmstrong/

MPI Learning *www.mpilearning.com*

Leading Others To Achieve Business Outcomes

Making The Complicated Happen
Why Leaders?

James Hall

Promise

Understand how to achieve complex things through groups of people using only simple, clear instructions.

Key Messages

- Harness the brilliance of your people; don't strangle their minds. Tell them 'what you want them to achieve', not how you want them to achieve it.

- Set objectives (with resources), don't just enforce processes and demand outcomes;

- Trust your people and help them to trust you: develop trust in the process.

My own personal definition of leadership is that it is *'the art of getting others to achieve things that they could or would not manage in the absence of the leader.'*

There are plenty of alternatives but this one works for me because it places the emphasis on the output of leadership effort.

Before I go any further I want to recognize and then park an issue that some readers may find worrying in the deductions from this definition. By using it, I may seem to suggest that the 'ends justify the means'. There is no doubt that history shows many examples of great leaders taking their people to bad places (you can insert your own historical bogey-man here).

Clearly modern leaders likely to be reading this do not intend to use their authority for negative reasons. We can park for another day a discussion of how we judge that outputs are 'the right ones' by noting that successful leaders who make bad judgements usually come to bad ends. Historical examples are numerous but commercially, you might think of the failure of Kodak to move from wet film to digital photography as a classic example of when a leadership team successfully took its people in the wrong direction, misunderstood changing technology and culture and ended in ruin.

Getting Things Done

What my definition does do is force us to focus on the outputs of leadership. I want to discuss how successful leaders get stuff done in a complicated world.

There are a couple of things we all intuitively know.

First, that any modern organization faces huge complexity and instability: micro and macro-economics change all the time; social and cultural assumptions move faster than ever before; technological opportunities come and go so that even the smallest business faces constant adjustments. Secondly, over-management does not work. We have all come across micro-managers and we know that, whilst usually honest and well-intentioned, they are hard to work for, hard to please and in practice lack the time or the skills to achieve what they intend. The truth is that few of us think of ourselves as micro-managers but most of us have, at one time or another, fallen into the trap. Why? Because, under pressure, it is hard to trust the team and feels easier to do it yourself. It's a short-term solution that never works in the long run.

Mission Leadership

I want to introduce you to a philosophy of leadership for getting complicated stuff done that is drawn from the doctrines of the NATO militaries. Don't be alarmed! This is simply a codification of an idea that most of us already aspire to, in which we try to enable our people to achieve their outputs through their own ingenuity rather than through micro-management.

The Military call this Mission Command. Since the civilian world is less comfortable with the idea of 'command' let's just call it 'Mission Leadership'. The idea is to get a lot of people and teams to work co-operatively to achieve shared objectives.

Where To Start

The trick to leading in this way lies in the following rules. Your people (all your people) need:

- to know the top level objective. Call it a purpose, mission, vision, objective or even 'Herbert' if you choose to. Whatever you call it, they need really to understand it.

- to know exactly the objectives of their immediate boss and why that objective matters.

- to grasp their own part in reaching the objective. What are they meant to achieve and, critically, why are they meant to achieve it?

- to trust their leaders and in turn, to be trusted to do the right thing in the right way using their own initiative, skills and ingenuity.

- the right resources to be made available.

By following these rules a simple instruction at the top can achieve immensely complex activity across the wider team. In a military example a General will say take your forces and capture this city so that at the lowest levels of the team hundreds or thousands of individuals rush to do their individual duties driving trucks, cooking meals or repairing equipment. The commercial world is no different: a CEO says get me into the US market and the whole organizational structure swings into action.

The Rules

This is how the military explains the philosophy. Remember, the idea is that at every level people will be enabled to use their own skills and initiative to do the right thing in the right way.

- The top level leader has a clear objective (mission) to achieve and several senior leaders who execute the plan. Each is given their own required output. Each of those outputs is designed in such a way that it enables other things to happen so that, when added together, they equal success in the top level mission.

- Next, each of those second level leaders plans how to achieve their own allocated output. They know why it must be achieved because they understand its part in the top level mission.

Each one of these leaders now turns to their own team at the third level to whom they give similar instructions.

- Now each of the third level leaders can see their own objective, together with that of their boss and the boss's boss....

... and so it goes on, a huge list of objectives cascading from top to bottom of the organization, a mass of individual instructions that run from General to Driver or from CEO to sales. It is a cohesive system of instructions in which people are told what they are to achieve and not how to do their job.

Let's look at the language of these instructions in a bit more detail.

Understanding My Objective And My Purpose

In this world, instructions sound like this. First I get the context. My boss will say to me:

'James, I have been asked by the CEO to get our sales turnover up by 10% by the end of the year. His purpose is to get the Company ready for sale to a new owner by March of next year. The Board has set a target of $550m valuation.'

In saying this I have been given the context of both my immediate boss and that of the levels above. Now I need to hear the instruction to me. It is structured like this:

'I want you to increase our sales conversion rate from 40 to 45% of enquiries' (*my objective*)

'...in order that I can increase our turnover by 10%.' (*my purpose and why my objective matters*)

'I am giving you £100 000 more in the budget to use as you see fit. I need you to get there by 31 December.' *(My resources and constraints).*

Perhaps the most important part of this instruction is the second – the why. Knowing this allows me to make judgements about my own task. Is my approach going to lead to success for my boss? Can I see a way in which to do a better job? In military parlance, is there an opportunity for me to seize the initiative to drive us towards the overall Mission?

How Do I Plan?

Now comes the point where I must work out my own plan to achieve my allocated output. This is where I work out my own 'how'.

First, I will analyse the instructions I have received. (The Military formally call this the Estimate process). From that analysis I will develop my own solution. At this point I must be given the chance to explain to my boss the results of my analysis and the implications of my plan. This back-brief process must be baked into any hierarchy of planning activity and be characterized by brutal honesty on both parts. This is my chance to say what I think, to negotiate more help where I need it and to point out risk.

'OK boss. I had a look. I see what you want and it's doable. That said, I've been thinking. To improve sales conversion rates, we need more time for the sales teams to spend with clients after we have made the offer. We need to improve contact with them during the decision making period. Can you help me with someone to bolster the teams at this point?'

Now I need the boss to think carefully before saying yes or no. Do I have a point? Is there another approach to offer me? I need to prove that, to achieve what is required, the extra resources are necessary. The boss needs to be certain I am right and to be willing to accept that a refusal means sharing responsibility should I under-perform.

Trust

This whole approach is about trust. In an organization where people talk honestly to one-another about their tasks and how to achieve them, success tends to follow. If I know you are aware of my problems, that you have done what you can to solve them and that you will support me as I work through them, then I am going to try harder and will be confident that we will share successes and failures equally.

Honesty in all this is critical. Those who hide risks, pass blame or pander to the hierarchy may succeed in the short term but their organisations seldom do.

Your People

Inevitably, your people are your key resource in this. Leading in this style means you have to nurture and support them in very specific ways. Should you treat all your staff in exactly the same way? No. An experienced team member can be allocated an output and resources and left to get on with it. A less experienced employee, someone new or lacking confidence, will need greater support and more direction. You still need to set the objectives and outputs and to demonstrate that you expect them to be achieved. The difference is that you need to take care to provide the right oversight and guidance to give the best chance of success.

Risk

This form of leadership is really about taking advantage of risk. Giving people the opportunity to think and act for themselves presents the chance of failure as well as success. Guiding team members to help them avoid failure whilst still allowing them to operate with freedom is the critical talent in a leader who adopts this philosophy.

Every leader I meet tells me they are willing to accept the risk of failure in order to encourage initiative. I am sure they all believe this but conversation with their people often suggests another side to the story. In any case, whilst failures do happen they should be rare. A successful leader will watch carefully to identify problems as they develop and be ready to step in with guidance and resources when needed.

Successful Situational Leadership

Successful situational leadership builds mutual trust between leader and led. It provides, not just resources and clear instructions, but advice and guidance and a sense of mutual responsibility for shared objectives. In doing so, it offers the chance for individuals and teams to flourish.

Finally, it is easy to become lost in the details of leadership and to agonise over the forms of words and the concepts around which instructions are woven. First and foremost, any form of leadership is about human relations. Success requires understanding, sensitivity and intelligence. In that sense, this way of describing leadership is no different from any other!

About JW Hall MBE MDA MA (Oxon) FCMI FCILM

James Hall has over forty years of military and commercial experience. His international work as a leader extends across the world from the Americas, to Nigeria and West Africa, Yemen, the Middle East and the Balkans. In more recent years he has worked to support the development of senior leaders in the world of corporate business. He admits privately to particularly enjoying working with those who run small and medium sized companies.

During the 2014 rebellion in Yemen, James was responsible for the leadership of several thousand commercial security guards as Houthi forces entered the capital city of Sana'a. This experience was the first time in which his experience of security operations was tinged with the cold realities of the commercial world. In previous years, while still serving as a British Army Officer, he had been responsible for hostage recovery and counter-terrorism operations in West Africa and had acted as Chief Instructor in the delivery of training in leadership and strategic planning to multi-national officers at the US Army's Command and Staff College.

Today, James delivers management and leadership training to all levels in multinational environments. He is particularly interested in businesses seeking to make better use of digital technologies and is a strong advocate for the use of data to strengthen the speed of quality decision making and change-management.

LinkedIn profile *www.linkedin.com/in/jameswilliamhall/*

MPI Learning *www.mpilearning.com*

Psychological Safety –
It's Real And It's Really Important

Nick Corbo

Promise

If you read this chapter, you'll understand what psychological safety is and why it's so critical that leaders today work to build it within their organisations.

Key Messages

- Psychological safety is a real phenomenon, and its origins can be linked to how our earliest ancestors formed groups

- The highest performing teams nurture psychological safety and the good news for leaders is that you can do the same

- In the current climate of economic and political instability, there are reasons why organisations must embrace building psychologically safe teams or risk severely underperforming

Working with an executive team recently, the topic of psychological safety came up in discussion, between two of the team members. I was asked my opinion and I eagerly replied that it was a subject very dear to my heart, having recently completed a research project on improving psychological safety in teams.

I was more than a little surprised when one of the team said that they didn't believe Psychological Safety was even real!

When asked if I was interested in contributing to this book, this brief conversation came to mind and I felt compelled to write about not only why psychological safety is very real, but also to share some thoughts about how as leaders we can enhance it in our teams, and why it matters. Let's start with the question of what psychological safety actually is.

What Is Psychological Safety?

Psychological safety is a phenomenon that people experience when in groups or teams. It has been described by a number of acclaimed authors, management thinkers and researchers. The term was first used by organisational change researchers, Edgar Schein and Warren Bennis (Schein and Bennis, 1965). Their observations suggested that in times of uncertainty, people would withhold their views as they associated some sort of risk with speaking in those moments, unless they could be assured of support from their peers. William Kahn made definitive links between psychological safety and an employee's engagement at work (Kahn, 1990), which makes absolute sense. How can you give your best and be truly engaged in any organisation where you feel unsure about giving your opinions and thoughts?

Possibly the most prominent writer on psychological safety is Harvard professor Amy Edmondson. She has written extensively on the subject, describing it as when people feel comfortable to share concerns, and mistakes without fear of retribution, being confident that when they speak up they will not be humiliated, ignored or blamed (Edmondson, 2018). If you have read that and think 'that's not my organisation', you may need to check that you're right.

To explain the origins of this phenomenon, let me take you back in time to our very earliest ancestors, roaming the savannahs and living in caves. Predators were all around, providing genuine threat to life so to survive we formed groups, which we might refer to now as tribes. We operated in groups as means of survival from the many threats to life. With predators and rival groups around us, being part of a group increased our chances of surviving considerably. As a consequence, we evolved biologically to work to cooperate in groups. This is described brilliantly in Matthew Liebereman's book, Social (Lieberman, 2013), his research is supported by others who endorse the theory that we are now hard wired to connect (Fishbane, 2007). Neurologically we reward ourselves when we trust others through the release of the feel good chemical oxytocin to encourage us to form groups (Zak, 2017), because it's so important to our survival. So, if we're wired to connect then why is there an issue? For that we need to go back to the tribes in their caves.

Imagine being a member of a tribe, you have strength in numbers, but you need to be accepted by the group and stay accepted by the group to remain safe. Most importantly you need acceptance from the tribe's leader. They have the power to exclude you from the group, effectively sealing your demise. That is going to affect how you behave in the group, right? Add to this, the fact that in those tribes, leaders were not elected democratically, the leader tended to be the biggest, strongest fiercest warrior. This would mean that in addition to having the power to exclude you from the group, they also had the physical power to bring you great harm if you were to upset them. If you had ideas or opinions about what the tribe should be doing, you'd want to be pretty certain that the tribe's leader would agree and not be angry with you or see you in a bad light, your very safety would depend on it.

These 'fears' have been passed on to us through our DNA and are at the heart of why psychological safety is an issue for all organisations. The innate fear some of us experience in speaking up to someone in a position of power comes from our ancestors' experiences. To finish painting the picture it's worth also knowing that as human beings we have adapted and evolved, as we always do, to ensure our future survival. Unfortunately this evolution took the form of ensuring that what we refer to now as 'social pain' created through social exclusion (from groups) is at least equal to the suffering we experience from physical pain, as demonstrated in the research carried out by Naomi Eisenberger (Eisenberger, 2012).

To summarise; we are hard wired to connect and work together in groups, we're also hard wired to experience pain when we are rejected in groups or excluded, and we have an innate fear of displeasing authority figures that now plays out in work teams and organisations in what has been referred to as implicit voice theories (Detert and Edmondson, 2011). If all of this is making you want to stop reading this chapter and throw your hands up in despair, don't…because as leaders you might just have the power to assuage these innate fears and help people feel really secure in their 'work tribes'. Before we discuss how, let's understand a little more about why creating high levels of psychological safety is so important.

Why Psychological Safety Matters

The simple answer is that for high performing teams it's essential. Google found this out through their own research project, 'Aristotle', which was designed to understand the most important factors in creating high performance teams. Different hypotheses were suggested including, finding the smartest people and putting them together and finding the most inspirational leaders. However, what emerged was quite unexpected and reported upon in the New York Times (Duhigg, 2016). A high level of psychological safety was deemed a critical factor in creating high performing teams. Think about that for a moment and it will make perfect sense. High performing teams are made up of people that are totally committed to achieving success, so committed that they are willing to be open about mistakes and learn from them, rather than hiding them from their leaders. They are also teams where every member feels able to give ideas and opinions, in fact these are welcomed by peers and leaders alike. Now, if this sounds like it's just about creating a nice place to work where everyone has their say, it's really not that at all. In addition to giving ideas and opinions, team members can expect to have their ideas and thinking challenged in the spirit of achieving the best result.

There is a huge impact when organisations don't get a diversity of views, providing their leaders with support and challenge to make the best decisions possible. Even more detrimental is when organisations don't get the real views of the people within it, a little like blood pressure is known as a silent killer, employee silence can be terminal for your organisation. The other similarity to blood pressure is that silence from your employees, withholding their ideas and thoughts, even hiding errors is that silence is clearly unseen, unheard and easily overlooked.

If you want evidence of the impact of low psychological safety, sadly there are several examples available. Perhaps the most high-profile example is the NASA Challenger disaster in 1986. With the shuttle programme under pressure to justify its huge expense the prospect of repeated delays to launches, particularly due to technical issues were unthinkable. However, an engineer at one of NASA's contractors suggested that the O-rings might malfunction in the extreme cold temperatures due on the day of the launch. The engineer's concerns were not raised to senior management, instead they were silenced, presumably due to the pressure of meeting the objectives and the potential response the bringer of bad news may receive. The result was catastrophic. A delay of launch and more time spent assessing the data around the faulty rings could have saved lives.

The Fukushima nuclear disaster in Japan 2011, could also have been avoided if warnings that the sea walls protecting the plant were not high enough, had been listened to. A 2006 report from Professor Katsuhiko predicted the potential disaster but was dismissed by a Japanese subcommittee tasked with reviewing nuclear plant safety standards. A number of advisors to the subcommittee had ties to the power companies, and rejected the claims, potentially fearful of the reaction from their leaders. A year later, Katsuhiko published a second report expressing his concerns and again was silenced. The effect was that when the sea walls were breached in 2011, compromising the safety of the plant, more than 400,000 people were displaced from their homes and the world faced its biggest nuclear accident since Chernobyl. Those 400,000 will never be able to return to their homes. In an environment where psychological safety was higher, warnings would have been investigated and this disaster would not have occurred.

These are extreme examples, but they are replicated in organisations across the globe. The impact may not be as devastating as costing lives but the impacts of leaders not having full information or data available, not having decisions challenged can mean that flawed thinking drives strategy.

If we acknowledge that leaders are not the font of all knowledge and I think that most of us do, then we also acknowledge that strong voices, ideas, challenges are required from those around leaders to help improve decision making. This is particularly true when organisations and teams are going through tough times or periods of real uncertainty. Now is just such a time. Uncertainty over the economic outlook abounds, trust in our political leaders wavers and the energy crisis are bringing unpredicted pressures on businesses and homes alike. All of this as we work our way through the tail end of a pandemic. In the UK alone, the BBC reported that 400,000 redundancies were made in just three months during the Covid 19 pandemic (King, 2021), a record high. Re-structures and 'right-sizing' have become common place in organisations across the globe as they deal with the huge challenges they have faced. Now consider how psychologically safe people in organisations will feel. The pressure to keep jobs and maintain status may never be higher for people and that could have a significant effect on behaviours at work. The effect could be to silence voices and for people to take the safe option of not speaking up or offering differences of opinion, the complete opposite of what you need for a high performing team.

Can You Improve Psychological Safety?

Let's give you some good news. Yes you can and there are some simple steps you can take to make a positive impact.

1. **Measure where you are now** From the research conducted by Amy Edmondson, there is a survey and method of measuring current levels of psychological safety among your teams (Edmondson, 1999). Creating a baseline will facilitate a discussion and begin the process for making improvements.

2. **Create a positive future vision of the team.** You want to be and take feedback from your team. Research has shown that working towards a positive future vision activates areas of the brain associated with engagement, building trust and regulating stress responses (Boyatzis and Jack, 2018). This is particularly helpful for creating a space where people will speak freely and provide feedback.

3. **Ask lots more questions.** Be more curious and encourage those around you to do the same. Simple enquiries around how people know that their recommendation is the best option, asking how a solution or decision could be improved further create an environment where thinking is stretched, and better decisions are made.

4. **Be open about challenges the team face and invite opinions and challenge.** Make sure that with your team you debate major decisions. Acknowledge that you may not have the right answer and you want to hear everyone's views. Research has shown that inclusive leadership and explaining why input from the team is so important is a key factor in building psychological safety in teams (Nembhard and Edmondson, 2006). One way to do this is to adopt a simple routine in meetings, suggested by Nancy Kline (Kline, 1999) where for every discussion point team members are given uninterrupted time to air their view. The uninterrupted part of this is key, anxiety over being

interrupted can be a silencer and knowing that you will be heard by your peers and leaders encourages participation.

It is absolutely possible to build and improve safety psychological safety in teams. It takes effort and it takes a degree of courage from leaders. Courage to be vulnerable and admit that you may not have all the answers, courage to admit that you might not have the best ideas and courage to accept mistakes and learn from them. This kind of courage builds teams and demonstrates belief in team members, it creates environments where people feel able to give of their best and it creates high performing teams.

References

- Boyatzis, R.E. and Jack, A.I. (2018) 'The neuroscience of coaching.', Consulting Psychology Journal: Practice and Research, 70(1), p. 11.

- Detert, J.R. and Edmondson, A.C. (2011) 'Implicit voice theories: Taken-for-granted rules of self-censorship at work', Academy of management journal, 54(3), pp. 461–488.

- Duhigg, C. (2016) 'What Google Learned From Its Quest to Build the Perfect Team', The New York Times, 25 February. Available at: https://www.nytimes.com/2016/02/28/magazine/what-google-learned-from-its-quest-to-build-the-perfect-team.html (Accessed: 23 July 2020).

- Edmondson, A. (1999) 'Psychological safety and learning behavior in work teams', Administrative science quarterly, 44(2), pp. 350–383.

- Edmondson, A.C. (2018) The Fearless Organization: Creating Psychological Safety in the Workplace for Learning, Innovation, and Growth. Illustrated edition. Hoboken, New Jersey: John Wiley & Sons.

- Eisenberger, N.I. (2012) 'The pain of social disconnection: examining the shared neural underpinnings of physical and social pain', Nature Reviews Neuroscience, 13(6), pp. 421–434.

- Fishbane, M.D. (2007) 'Wired to connect: Neuroscience, relationships, and therapy', FAMILY PROCESS-CALIFORNIA THEN NEW YORK–, 46(3), p. 395.

- Kahn, W.A. (1990) 'Psychological conditions of personal engagement and disengagement at work', Academy of management journal, 33(4), pp. 692–724.

- King, B. (2021) 'Unemployment rate: How many people are out of work?', BBC News, 26 January. Available at: https://www.bbc.com/news/business-52660591 (Accessed: 30 January 2021).

- Kline, N. (1999) Time to think: Listening to ignite the human mind. Hachette UK.

- Lieberman, M.D. (2013) Social: Why our brains are wired to connect. Oxford, United Kingdom: OUP Oxford.

- Nembhard, I.M. and Edmondson, A.C. (2006) 'Making it safe: The effects of leader inclusiveness and professional status on psychological safety and improvement efforts in health care teams', Journal of Organizational Behavior: The International Journal of Industrial, Occupational and Organizational Psychology and Behavior, 27(7), pp. 941–966.

- Schein, E.H. and Bennis, W.G. (1965) Personal and Organizational Change. New York: John Wiley & Sons Ltd.

- Zak, P.J. (2017) 'The neuroscience of trust', Harvard Business Review, 95(1), pp. 84–90.

About Nick Corbo

Nick is a freelance management consultant, executive coach and facilitator. He has an extensive senior management background in operational leadership and senior L&D roles. His experience has included integration of teams following major mergers, acquisition and relocation of business and design and delivery of  major leadership development programmes in a FTSE 250. He has particular experience and expertise in contact centre operations, insurance, financial services and travel. His most recent projects include working with; Tesco Bank, Great Western Railways, Royal Pharmaceutical Society, Riviera Travel, IC24 and Andrews Property Group.

He has an MBA from the University of Leicester and an MSc in Coaching and Behavioural Change from Henley Business School, where his research project explored the efficacy of team coaching in improving psychological safety in work teams.

LinkedIn *linkedin.com/in/nick-corbo-436192174*

MPI Learning *www.mpilearning.com*

Leading Small Teams

James Hall

Promise

Think more carefully about the leadership required to make small teams High Performing

Key Messages

- The power of the High Performing Team

- Leading small teams requires some different skills

- Finding the future leaders of big organisations from amongst successful HPTs

I am sure that at some point you have yourself some version of these questions:

Will someone who is good at running a medium sized technology company automatically be right to take over my medium sized hospital; or, will a junior board member, brilliant at running an eight-man team charged with developing next generation products be equally successful when promoted to lead the corporation?

We have all seen it happen.

Someone does well through their career, succeeding in task after task and job after job as they battle for the top. At some stage all too many reach a point of failure. At that point it is easy for the cynical to assume that they have been over-promoted. In truth though, the chances are that the person was never fully trained or prepared to make the transition from one style of leadership to another.

This article is about the specific skills required to run a small team. The general point is simple. The requirements of successful leadership change with the environment and one size does not fit all. Since organisations require effective leadership skills to be exercised at all levels it seems obvious that we should think very hard about identifying the right people for the right role and then giving them the right skills.

'In The Old Days Leaders...'

Before I go too much further, I want to emphasise what seems to me an obvious point but which I think is important. Some leadership skills are timeless. We can and should learn from our predecessors.

If you have not read about Alexander the Great or Henry Ford or other great examples then I urge you to do so with an open mind. We learn from them simply because the human brain is hard wired and evolution moves slowly! You can probably list your version of resulting fundamental characteristics of leadership for yourself: my own would include concepts like confidence, clarity of purpose, and emotional intelligence. Good leaders should make a point of studying the past as well as the present if they are to develop their skills.

On the other hand, it is equally obvious that these fundamental characteristics are expressed in very different ways in different environments. Studying leadership has shown me very clearly that each generation must adapt to the circumstances of the moment.

The High Performing Team (HPT)

One particular specialisation is studied much less than I think it should be: small team leadership. Small teams exist amidst all levels of large organisations. They are groups who must work tightly together to achieve unified aims and where the sum of their individual efforts should be considerably greater than the contributions of their individual components. In the jargon of the coaching world, these are High Performing Teams (HPT).

Being part of an HPT can be a fantastic experience. For a business they can be critical to success because their achievements massively outweigh their cost and scale. Time and effort in developing them is never wasted.

I have been lucky enough to be part of several, first with the Armed Forces and more recently as a consultant working for a small company in the Middle East. Multi-national, multi-cultural and oddly composed of people of remarkable diversity of thought and background, we melded together to produce results of which no-one had expected us to be capable. Our leader was magnificent, primarily because no outside visitor was ever able to identify who it was. His presence was real to us and critical to our output, but he was well hidden amongst the group. We existed and succeeded because the company saw the power of the group and worked hard to enable it.

What Makes A Team High Performing?

You will probably have been part of a small team yourself, whether High Performing or not. Perhaps you were one of a group brought together to run a project with a clearly defined output. Perhaps you are on the main board of a large manufacturing company.

These teams may all be very different in their outputs but, to succeed, their members need to share some fundamental characteristics and assumptions:

- These teams may all be very different in their outputs but, to succeed, their members need to share some fundamental characteristics. First, they need to be small enough to form a cohesive human unit. In my experience this means somewhere between four and perhaps ten people. Many more than that and it simply becomes impossible to work sufficiently closely with your peers..

(Importantly, this is not about the idea of 'team' as leaders of big organisations tend to use the word. 'We are all one Team now' yells the CEO to his 25 000 employees. Nice point, but not what I am describing).

Members of a HPT must also share an absolute understanding of:

- the overall objective. What they are trying to achieve;
- and the route by which they intend to get there.

In addition, they must share a common approach:

- a willingness to divide the labour equally amongst them.
  In an HPT it is vital that 'my problem is your problem'.
  You may run sales and I may do finance but we share a unified
  goal and I will help you as best I can. I will be confident that
  you will do the same for me;

- a willingness to share success and failure. 'One in, all in';

- absolute trust and honesty. I really should not need to say
  more to an audience that thinks about leadership!

Teams That Underperform

Just as it is great to be part of an HPT, it is awful to be part of
one which is failing. If you have never been part of a dysfunctional
group, masquerading as a team then take my word for it. Distrust,
fear, overt-dislike, internal politics, selfishness – the list of human
nastiness rapidly begins to feel unlimited and characteristics that
none of us ever see in ourselves suddenly become manifest in
those around us.

The Small Team Leader

Leading a small team under these circumstances therefore first
requires all the characteristics of any other form of leadership.
One must be confident. One must be clear about objectives.
One must be seen to care both for the output and the other team
members.

Beyond that though, there are specific demands that are
peculiar to the environment and understanding them depends on

possessing a wider knowledge of what moves a team from being dysfunctional to High Performing.

First, the Team needs to know what it is doing and where it is going and its members must be united in an absolute belief in the approach adopted to get there. This is not the same as nodding at the boss and smiling whilst you mutter rude words under your breath! Nor is it the same as the general level of cohesion expected of a larger group. This is about close co-operation between individuals where each genuinely shares the minutiae and an emotional attachment to the agreed output and approach.

In an HPT, team members need to know and trust their fellows implicitly: how they think, their likes and dislikes, strengths and weaknesses. They must share in success and failure whilst at the same time being honest about problems, mistakes and underperformance. They must also share in the hard work. Free-loaders and observers will not succeed and will destroy the cohesion of the group.

To control and enable this lot, a leader needs to understand and encourage these characteristics. A small team leader, whilst exercising real authority, usually presents not as the 'one at the top' but as the 'first amongst equals'. That means doing real work on behalf of the group, not merely getting other people to do it for you. It means sitting with your people as one of them and yet, at the same time, exercising influence, often by very indirect means.

What kind of a person does this suit? As an extrovert, it pains me to admit that my style is not always best suited to this. Extroverts can be brilliant at the role, but the HPT leader must be a listener, a 'belonger', an influencer who shares in the joys and takes on board the failures of the team and all its members. I claim to be able to do that stuff – but I have to work at listening skills!

How Does It Feel To Work For An HPT Leader?

The answer is that output genuinely soars around you. It will be obvious because your fellows are consistently working at top level, not for themselves but for you and for the overall objective. Mutual reliance, respect and responsibility suddenly seems real between you all. Oddly, no-one is obviously at the core and no-one is left out. Indeed one of the great challenges can be when a member leaves and the whole structure becomes unbalanced. The HPT leader is a powerful presence but always as someone who acts from within rather than above the group.

Leading Big Numbers

It must be obvious now that the skills to deliver this kind of leadership are not necessary the same as that needed for leading at a larger scale. The CEO who controls thousands of people cannot be personally connected to each and every one, cannot share their thoughts, their methods, and their personal successes and failures. The senior leader can never just be 'primus inter pares' of the wider team.

Which is not to argue that the leader of a large organisation has to be a shouty, noisy extrovert – even though all too often they are. To influence large numbers of people requires huge sensitivity, a macro understanding of the culture of the organisation and its components, and an ability to react to its needs, to communicate in ways which work for the audience and to demonstrate real trust and clarity.

Most of us suspect that far too many people go too high up their hierarchies because they are noisy self-publicists. We all know of examples where noise and bluster succeeds. Sometimes that noise covers real capability and that should be welcomed. All too often though, it masks weakness and hides the value of equally competent but less brash colleagues.

A Suggestion

A great many very successful and capable people (mostly extroverts) are going to find it initially very hard to run a High Performing Team. In order to do so, they will need to make significant changes to their style. Importantly though, this form of leadership can be taught and developed. With the right guidance and the right people the magic of the HPT can be coaxed from a group and the resulting value will be significant for the wider organisation. With a bit of help, people not naturally suited to the role of small team leadership may suddenly find that the skills they learn in this environment greatly help them when they move on to larger challenges.

Most of us worry that we sometimes select the wrong leaders. I imagine most of us also agree that the style of leadership adopted must always be adapted to the particular needs of the environment.

In searching for someone to run a small team, you are looking for a very specific set of characteristics. Neither an introvert nor an extrovert, but someone whose skill is to work from within rather that from above.

On the other hand, when looking for the next CEO or (given

the date of writing, in Autumn 2022, the next Prime Minister), you might do well to look amongst your successful small team leaders to see whether there is a person, perhaps overshadowed by more noisy brethren, who would suit higher positions. The skills of an HPT leader can be highly transferable.

My recommendation is to work to develop and nurture your small team leaders. Not only will the output they achieve astonish you, but you will find amongst them gold standard potential for the larger challenges of running your wider business.

About JW Hall MBE MDA MA (Oxon) FCMI FCILM

James Hall has over forty years of military and commercial experience. His international work as a leader extends across the world from the Americas, to Nigeria and West Africa, Yemen, the Middle East and the Balkans. In more recent years he has worked to support the development of senior leaders in the world of corporate business. He admits privately to particularly enjoying working with those who run small and medium sized companies.

During the 2014 rebellion in Yemen James was responsible for the leadership of several thousand commercial security guards as Houthi forces entered the capital city of Sana'a. This experience was the first time in which his experience of security operations was tinged with the cold realities of the commercial world. In previous years, while still serving as a British Army Officer, he had been responsible for hostage recovery and counter-terrorism operations in West Africa and had acted as Chief Instructor in the delivery of training in leadership and strategic planning to multi-national officers at the US Army's Command and Staff College.

Today, James delivers management and leadership training to all levels in multinational environments. He is particularly interested in businesses seeking to make better use of digital technologies and is a strong advocate for the use of data to strengthen the speed of quality decision making and change-management.

LinkedIn *www.linkedin.com/in/jameswilliamhall/*

MPI Learning *www.mpilearning.com*

Five Steps To Leading A Stickier Business

Andy Goram

Promise

This chapter will inspire you to take some simple steps to start building a stickier business. A place where people love to work, where they thrive, stay and attract more great talent to you.

Key Messages

- Being sticky takes more than paying a fair wage

- The simple steps you can take to build a stickier business

- True stickiness takes commitment and consistency

I was a marketing leader for 27+ years. I spent millions trying to understand my customers and get them to buy from me, stay with me, do more things with me and recommend me to others. I'm ashamed to say that it wasn't until the latter part of my marketing career that I put as much focus on engaging my internal audience with similar goals. But when I did, the results were quite astonishing.

In this chapter I will share with you the simple steps, based on my experiences and learning, you should take as a leader, to engage and retain more of your people, helping you build a more magnetic employer brand and lay the foundations for a sustainably successful and enabling culture. That's what I call, a stickier business. The sort of place where people love to work, where they thrive, stay and attract more great talent to you, and where more customers stay with you and recommend you to others because they also love what you do and how you do it.

First things first. To begin your journey to stickiness paying an employee fairly is just a table stake. If you don't do that in the first place, don't be surprised if you are losing people for pence and pounds on the hourly rate that someone else offers down the road. You cannot sustainably compete in today's people market on salary alone. Today, people are demanding more. Especially the new working generation. You have to engage on a deeper level if you want to hold on to more of your talent.

The challenge of employee engagement can seem like an overwhelming and a never-ending pursuit. The thing is that's right in one regard. It is never-ending. Engaging your people enough to keep them and performing at their best isn't a one-off job. It's a constant. I wouldn't have dreamed of switching off the focus on my customers as a marketer, to keep them engaged, so why should it be any different with your people?

In my experience there are five key steps to lighting the fires within your people. Some of them are backed up in David MacLeod and Nita Clarke's 'Engaging For Success' UK Government report[1]. The thing is, by doing these things, you'll also increase the value and perception of your employer brand, making your organisation more attractive to new talent. The secrets lie in connecting what drives your people, with what drives the business.

Step 1: Create and tell your business' engaging story.

Your business' engaging story needs to be an authentic story, told from the leader's personal perspective, that conveys where the business has come from, where it's going, why it needs to go there and what it's going to take to do that.

But do your people really need a story? Yes, they do. As humans, we're not great at dealing with uncertainty. Having a story, that's told consistently, shows where you're headed, illustrates how your people play their part in delivering the outcome and why it matters, well, it all helps them to feel more certain. If it's just a story about how shareholders will benefit, it won't work (unless they are all shareholders!) because it doesn't show what's in it for them. Don't gloss over the detail either. Just because you've spent ages iterating and condensing it, don't leave out the why behind it all. That's the bit that helps your audience connect to it and take ownership for it.

I saw the magic of doing this well, right before my eyes a few years ago while working in Hospitality. I was out with some Board members one day; on the back of a big re-brand we were executing. We landed in a venue and a member of the Board decided they wanted to have a look back of house. The rest of the Board followed. As a succession of suits piled into the narrow hallway that led to the colleague area, a wall that had our rebranding mission on it grabbed their attention. As I stepped up to explain what this was saying, a young Assistant Manager, Colleen, came into view down the corridor. Another Board member immediately pounced on Colleen and said, 'So what's all this about then?' I physically gulped. All my hours of planning and storytelling lay in the hands of Colleen. What would she say? I held my breath. But what happened, crystalised my belief in this step. She went on to tell the perfect story of the brand journey we were on. It was her take on it. It was personal. It was authentic. It was aligned to the venue actions scrawled on the board, and it was probably far better than I would have told it. She was brilliant.

The looks and nods from the Board told me all I needed to know. People clearly got this, connected with it, understood what it would take to deliver the vision and how they played their part in that. The time I'd spent running around the country telling the story, getting them to play it back and tell their own versions had paid dividends. Nothing's more powerful than a good story for transferring ownership for behaviour.

Step 2: Know yourself and find personal connections with your people.

The second step is about enabling your managers and leaders to build and manage trust in their teams. But what does that mean, and how do you do that?

Firstly, this is about building self-awareness. It's hard to lead others effectively until you properly understand yourself, your behaviour, motivations and the impact that has on others. It's only then, through making genuine, personal connections, you can build successful, strong working relationships which lay the foundations for trust. And you, as a leader, need to give them the support, tools and training to do so. This is the bedrock on which high-performing teams that I've worked in were built on.

On the podcast I host, *Sticky From The Inside*, I heard a great story from one of my guests which illustrated how simple it can be to authentically get to know your team and build trust. In his research into effective teams, he'd come across a team that could not speak highly enough of their leader. The team were effusive in their praise of how well she knew them, had their back and pushed them to succeed. When he asked her what her secret was, she looked embarrassed. She reached down into a well-used Tote bag beside her and pulled out a worn notebook. 'Here's my secret', she said. 'Whenever I spoke to any of my team about their personal lives, or what was going on with them, I made a little note in this book, because I have a terrible memory. Over the weeks and months, it helped me build a real understanding of them, but it also prompted me to ask how Johnny had got on with his exams, or if Heather had recovered from her illness.'

Connecting with her employees on a personal level, with the help of a simple notebook, established a stable platform of trust. She doesn't really need the book anymore, but it's become a hard habit to break.

Intentionally building personal connections lays the foundations for trust. How are you role-modelling and encouraging this with your people and teams?

Step 3: Listen and respond to your employees' voice.

When employees feel like they have a voice that is listened to, understood and where appropriate, acted upon, it makes them feel like they matter. This is about setting up the formal and informal listening and conversation mechanics in the business.

The thing is, if you're going to ask for comment, have the courtesy to respond to the challenging stuff as well as the easy things. If you were having a conversation with someone, and you asked for their opinion on something, but you didn't agree with them, would you then just blank them? No! You'd respond explaining why you have a different point of view. Why should it be any different with your people?

I've run various engagement and listening programmes on both client and the consulting side, and the most enlightening stuff is always contained in the verbatim comments. These are the gold that help you to unlock any poor scores and retention rates. As soon as I see phrases like 'I don't know why I'm bothering to respond to this survey. Nothing ever happens, and no-one ever responds to my comments', I know we're seeing the consequences of a tick-box approach to engaging with the workforce.

In one company I worked in, I had a guy in HR Audit, who regularly sent me promotional ideas. Many of them were mad, crazy and wholly impractical. Every time he sent one through I either popped round to thank him and talk him through why we couldn't execute this particular idea or dropped him an email to the same effect. He was always grateful for the explanation, and the ideas kept on coming. I could've chosen to ignore him; I was very busy. But we had asked for ideas, so what message would that have sent? Eventually, one day, he sent through a cracker. Well, if I'm being honest, an idea that spawned a cracker of a promotion. If I'd have ignored him and shut him down, I'm sure I would've missed that idea. If you are opening the channels for dialogue, you must keep them open, and show you value their input, or risk people not bothering, disengaging and missing out on cracking ideas!

Step 4: Match the promise to the reality.

How do the promises you make about how the company operates and what it feels like to be part of it, match up to reality?

What's your culture really like now, and what does it need to be to succeed going forwards? How honest about that are you?

If you really value people working through the night and weekends, and want to appeal to that kind of folk, don't say that you're all about work-life balance. It's about making sure that the core values the business holds true and the behaviours that actually exist, align consistently, and contribute actively to the mission of the business and add real value to your employees, every day. If they don't, change them.

Leaders have to show that these values and behaviours are important through their consistent actions, not just words, it's just as important as the financial metrics many leaders happily review each day.

Of course, it's about reinforcing and celebrating where you see aligned behaviours, but it is also just as important to nip the unhelpful behaviours in the bud, or you risk nullifying the positive benefits of these things. This step is the one I had to learn most about. I was always a strong advocate for the values, but I let people down by not holding 'good performers' to account for out of line behaviours. This weakened their importance and showed others that the efforts they were making to keep the values alive weren't worth it. Like a reformed smoker, I cringe at my past behaviour, and now campaign for rehabilitation.

Values are a wonderful force for good if they match up to reality. Are your values relevant, alive and adding value to your organisation? If they don't and you're not going to face up to that, you're better off not having them.

Step 5: Wrap it all up in consistent, engaging communications.

Finally, you need to wrap it up in clear, consistent, relevant, and engaging communication, that never lets up. I guess you'd expect that from a marketing guy, wouldn't you?

You don't retain and engage your people with a tsunami of one-off blasts of information downloads, or the broadcast of random, seemingly unrelated comms pieces.

This is about finding and using the right channels, to have the appropriate dialogue with your employees, with the goal of keeping them informed and involved in the progress the business is making in the pursuit of its mission you spoke of in that story.

It's about consistently aligning all the various messages people receive, back to the story, values and strategy. Creating and sustaining an ongoing conversation about where we're headed, how we're doing, how people are contributing and what's next.

If I look back to that rebranding job at the start of this chapter, that's what we did. We were relentless in the focus of our communication and linking it back to the story, values and strategy. It's why Colleen was able to talk confidently about the vision for her business and the brand, and be very clear about what was needed to deliver that.

It wasn't until I thought about how and why I communicated with customers, and I applied that thinking and effort to our internal teams, that I started to see the lights go on behind people's eyes and get a sense that they really got where we were going, why we were going there and most importantly the role they played in that. Do you spend as much effort communicating internally, as you do externally? If not, why not?

So that's my five steps to stickiness. A simple path to begin retaining more of your great talent and being more attractive to new people. Hopefully it's demystified the challenge and given you a simple pathway to follow.

The road to stickiness starts with you. If there's one thing I've learned with any form of culture change or development, it's that you have to be the change you seek. Be the pebble that's thrown in the water. Don't wait to be one of the ripples. This stuff works for whole organisations, but it works in smaller teams too. Whatever your role, start where you have most control and influence and go from there. I promise you, take these five steps and stickiness and all the benefits that brings is just around the corner.

Reference

1. MacLeod, David and Clarke, Nita, Department for Business, Innovation and Skills (BIS), corp creator. (2011) Engaging for success: enhancing performance through employee engagement, a report to Government.

About Andy Goram

Andy Goram is an employee engagement and culture transformation consultant with experience across Leisure, Hospitality, Retail, Care, Medical Services, Fintech, Manufacturing, Training & Development and Not-for-Profit sectors. He's known and valued for being an energetic, effective and empathetic facilitator, sound strategic thinker, and strong communicator.

For over 25 years, Andy worked in various senior brand and corporate marketing roles. Working as the strategic conduit between Marketing, HR, and Operations departments he ensured that everything aligned to and helped improve the culture of the business, the brand reputation, was practically deliverable on the front line and delivered brilliant outcomes for customers, profitably.

He's also the host of the popular employee engagement, culture and human leadership podcast Sticky From The Inside. He's also an active volunteer with Engage for Success, the UK's leading voice on employee engagement and is a co-host of their long-running Engage For Success Radio Show.

LinkedIn *www.linkedin.com/in/andygoram/*

MPI Learning *www.mpilearning.com*

Inclusive Leadership:
Look Through A Different Lens

Ellen J. Burton

The Promise

After reading this chapter you will understand how you can positively impact your team and organization by practicing the skills and awareness essential to becoming an inclusive leader.

Bias, Beliefs, And Blind Spots:
How To Really See What's Going On

Even the most experienced leaders can be oblivious to disrespectful interactions at work. Unexplored bias leaves leaders with blind spots, making it difficult to register the detriment of exclusionary behavior among employees. Once aware, you will better recognize destructive interactions and learn to tactfully disrupt them.

Bias is a neurological function wherein the brain, completely subconsciously, constantly, and quickly, categorizes all new stimuli with a primary focus of distinguishing threats from everything else.

Once safety is confirmed and relevant information is retained, the brain sorts and files away this information to be retrieved when needed. Bias can be for positive thoughts and feelings, or for a negative 'story' you quickly tell yourself – this person, place, or thing is a threat (negative).

For example: imagine you are the hiring manager and the first impression you have of a younger job candidate is that they dress appropriately, but quite different than you, have multiple piercings, and are therefore not a good fit. Within seconds, your brain makes the decision to discredit or devalue everything the candidate says because clearly, *'they're not a good fit!'* This type of bias refers to the 'Horns' effect. Unconscious bias can work in reverse too. The 'Halo' effect is when the candidate appeals to you because your brain quickly decides a candidate is relatable, familiar, so are a good fit because they dress in a way that you expect or speak with a familiar and comforting accent or dialect. In which case, because of that split second decision, you only consider things the candidate says that affirm your initial decision of their good 'fit.'

As an aside, the growing practice of relinquishing the concept of 'fit' strongly supports leaders who intend to develop a diverse workforce.

Even the most seasoned leaders can experience unconscious biases. For example, when a leader repeatedly observes a male employee interrupting and speaking over a female employee during team meetings, the impact of that gender-based implied disrespect may not register because of the leader's blind spot (unaware/oblivious/unmindful). Worse, blind spots may inhibit that leader from understanding the damage this show of disrespect and disregard may have on the woman, as well as the other team members. Studies show that when trust and a feeling of belonging are damaged, the result is a decrease in collaboration, creative problem solving, and innovation.

As you can imagine, when leaders are unaware that their brain is making quick judgments based on old and new beliefs, media input, academic experience, professional experience, stereotypes, prejudice, and the opinions of others, conclusions can be incorrect. The leader will make decisions without ever questioning why they believe what they believe, or why they like or dislike certain information/people/ideas. This can be detrimental to decision making, one of the key responsibilities of all leaders.

To make your unconscious biases conscious, practice slowing down and questioning your first thought. Next, drop the belief that you should be able to control your initial neurological filing system: its primary purpose is to keep you safe and manage the overload of data that comes to you daily. Again, you are not responsible for your first thought, but you are responsible for learning to question your first thought and you are definitely responsible for your decisions and actions.

Practice questioning your beliefs. You will find that some are relevant and work for you and some are inherited and no longer make sense. You will find that as a leader you'll learn to recognize your first belief: 'this type of debate and word-play is good teamwork and fosters powerful solutions.'

Next step, you will slow down and question that belief. What may appear is a new perspective; an opportunity to see the interactions in a different way as if you're wearing a new pair of glasses. You would see the female employee's frustration, anger, or disappointment with the coworker's disrespect, and with leadership's inability to control the tone of the meeting.

They may see the interrupting male's anger and frustration as well. Once this practice becomes part of you, you will have a better idea of when and how to intervene to cultivate respect and dignity in employee interactions.

The Benefits of Bifocals! From Anti-Racist To Allyship.

Most leaders now understand that identifying as 'anti-racist' is inadequate when the leader's desire is to have an equitable, respectful, and productive workplace. We'll magnify the practices which take you from anti-racist to ally, allowing you to know how to speak up when observing disrespect or disregard.

Once you get to a certain age, you'll realize you might be able to see without bifocals, but you'll have to squint, and squinting is exhausting. Without a new pair of glasses – a little help to see more clearly – you will not only become less effective as a leader, but a detriment to your organization. The way we work and interact with others has forever changed. To remain relevant, leaders must try looking at the workplace and its employees in a different way.

In the past, being against racism and systems that take away others' dignity and freedom would have been considered sufficient. But being against something is not the same as being for something – being an ally. Being against violence towards Asian-Americans or noticing a lack of management opportunities for black or brown employees, for example, would fall under the category of anti-racism. What is required of all in leadership today is willingness to grow from being anti-racist to becoming an ally for fairness and justice, especially in the workplace.

In the descriptions below you may recognize the stage you're in currently, as you grow from anti-racist to bystander to advocate and to ally:

- **Anti-racist:** This leader has blinders on. They may be actively or passively anti-racist. Their blind spots keep them uneducated about the business benefit of a diverse workforce and of the journey, issues, or challenges of their employees. This leader may not exhibit much empathy and does not understand that neutrality has a net-negative effect.

- **Bystander:** This professional has awareness of social issues and believes in fairness. This leader may witness an interaction of disregard or disrespect at work, and while having the desire to, doesn't feel they are able to intervene in the moment. They may have an emotional reaction to the interaction and sometimes it may take a while (hours or days) to register the interaction as inappropriate. This leader feels social issues are happening to others and they feel no personal responsibility to correct the situation or underlying system.

- **Advocate:** This is a leader with a strong set of values for justice, equity (equal opportunities and support), and fairness. They are well-intentioned and well-informed. They practice emotional intelligence, especially empathy. They invite opinions and suggestions for a more inclusive workplace. They know what they see when they observe a disrespectful incident, for example, the telling of a 'blonde joke' or someone mocking another employee's disability (different ability). This leader has developed a skill which gives them a sense of appropriate timing to support the target of the bullying and/or correct the behavior of the offender in a courageous conversation.

- **Ally:** This leader understands the business benefits of a diverse workforce but doesn't rest there. This is the leader who can assess equity opportunities and development programs within the organization. They are fully committed to initiating Employee Resource Groups (EGR) for under-supported employees and/or mentorship programs. This leader is humbled by 'needing bifocals' and learning a new way of leading, is aware of their biases, and is vocal about, and makes decisions based on, that humility and awareness. This professional challenges policies and practices that exclude others and is persistent in bringing the organization into a new and inclusive way of working.

Visualize Dignity

Imagine a workplace where every employee knows they belong! You'll appreciate ways to creatively apply established leadership skills in becoming an inclusive leader. The result of your vision: increased loyalty, employee effectiveness, and retention.

Visualization is a proven performance tool long used by athletes to lower anxiety and improve focus, resulting in peak performance. For the business leader, visualizing an emotionally safe workplace where everyone is appreciated for their diverse cultures, backgrounds, skills, and perspectives will function as a guide for sustained culture shift. Equitable and inclusive workplaces do not happen without executives' leaders, and supervisors committing to the practices of inclusive leadership.

I love seeing the relief in a coaching client's eyes when they realize becoming an inclusive leader doesn't have to be a heavy lift; That it is possible to apply existing leadership skills with a twist. For instance, during team meetings, visualize yourself as the Inclusive Leadership Coach! No need to show favoritism, every member of the team has value, you've been trained to challenge members to their best innovative ideas, solutions and performance.

But this can only happen if expectations are clear, and you hold everyone accountable.

More about meetings: the winningest Coach's meetings start on time, end on time, have clearly stated intentions, last either 20 or 50 minutes, and make clear the guidelines for engagement. The Coach instructs participants to speak one at a time, respect each other's experience and ideas, collaborate, and cooperate. Remember that the best sports coaches control internal competition so that their team members are at peak and most effective against a rival.

Or imagine you are the host of your department, extending courtesy and comfort to all your guests. A graceful host uses employees' names as a powerful inclusive leadership skill. In 'How to Win Friends and Influence People', Dale Carnegie wrote: 'Remember that a person's name is to that person the sweetest and most important sound in any language.' And so, it is with pronouns.

As part of your vision of an emotionally safe workplace, you naturally empower employees to show up as their whole selves, which may include their request for the way they prefer to be addressed and acknowledged, by name or pronouns for example. Viewing the work world through old glasses, not accepting things like sexual orientation and gender identification, will exhaust you and break down trust and loyalty in employees. It's OK if you don't agree with why some employees want to be addressed with different pronouns, but any good host will know that all humans want to matter and be respected. This show of grace and generosity builds loyalty and respect. Employees who feel their leader has their back will go the extra mile for them!

The same way you're used to asking for pronunciation of names you're not familiar with, your willingness to model the same courtesy to employees with different pronouns will only serve your leadership effectiveness in the long run. Yes, you're going to misspeak and make mistakes. If (when) you mistakenly use a pronoun based on your perception of a person's gender identity, and you see their blanched reaction, apologize, and humbly ask for a reminder of their preferred pronoun. We're all learning.

Finally, when interviewing for open positions, be curious and aware of your biases. For instance, if your hobby is golf and the employee being considered for promotion to a client facing position's hobby is skateboarding, be aware of the 'story' you might be telling yourself: 'An adult who plays with skateboards can't very be professional!'. Becoming more aware of the 'story' you tell yourself may prevent the mistake of passing on a valuable new hire. These leadership skills help you to be more inclusive, making you a winning coach and admired host. Your new glasses show you clearly how to welcome new employees, and make sure they not only feel expected, but also respected, on their first day and every day after.

Ultimately, having hired a diverse workforce is not enough. Organizations must follow through. Organizations that intentionally hire and develop diverse candidates, providing equitable opportunities for advancement and making sure their leadership team is trained to be inclusive, experience greater employee loyalty, increased retention and outperform projected revenue year over year.

About Ellen J. Burton

An international lecturer and subject matter expert on workplace culture, Ellen is also the author of the Amazon Best Seller, The Civility Project: How to build a culture of reverence to improve wellness, productivity, and profit.

Ellen and her associates provide solutions to the most prominent stressors on organizations: bullying, disrespect and disregard contributing to 'The Great Resignation'. EJB's solution: Support executive leaders clarifying their beliefs about expected employee's behavior; solidify those beliefs into policy; facilitate education and awareness sessions; support HR developing inclusive language on job postings; provide Inclusive Leadership Coaching; and aid in formation of a Cultural/ Diversity Committee.

Result: A sustained respectful, inclusive workplace experiencing decreased turnover, productive conflict management and increased attraction to high talent.

As Executive Coach, Ellen supports C-suite executives and executive directors to their professional goals. Those who coach with Ellen report improved focus, influence, capacity, work/life balance and results.

LinkedIn *www.linkedin.com/in/ellen-burton-she-her-0702289/*

MPI Learning *www.mpilearning.com*

Leading Others

The Imposter Phenomenon
And Turning Self-Doubts to Self-Beliefs

Vanessa Boon

Promise

Learn self-belief techniques for you, and the team you are nurturing. Free people from the doubts that hold them back to unlock untapped potential for business success.

Key Messages

- Identify the doubts – notice what your inner critic is saying and assess the credibility of the source.

- Challenge the doubts – make the case against the False Evidence Appearing Real (F.E.A.R) and develop evidence-based self-beliefs to replace them with.

- Don't overdo it – humility makes for good leaders.

· Why Does This Matter?

An estimated 70%[1] of people will experience the imposter phenomenon, with feelings of inadequacy. Fostering a culture of greater self-belief supports you and your workforce to 'take the brakes off' releasing fresher, braver, more creative ideas.

Some doubt, in comparison to arrogance, can be healthy, but when self-doubt becomes dominant it can be problematic. The effects can be draining, inhibiting potential, leading to indecision, overwhelm, ineffectiveness, anxiety and burnout. Imagine the transformation possible for you and your business with people set free from these doubts and fears. So, let's tune in to your inner chatter, that little voice that says things like 'I can't do this.' Together, we shall explore the context and sources of self-doubts leading to three practical steps:

- Identify the doubts
- Challenge the doubts
- Keep things in balance

A Context Of Keeping Up

With the fast-paced world of business, social media comparisons and ever-faster technological change, many people are feeling the strain. There are many demands on our time; when we suffer under the illusion that we can do it all that pressure can be experienced as stress.

Societal judgement, validation and pressure to perform can feel heavy, for example, in the role of leader, breadwinner, working parent, 'the responsible one', 'the strong one'. There is a sense of needing to live up to some unreachable standard. A need not only to do well but also to be seen to be doing well, on social media. It can feel like an impossible strain to match up to the seemingly flawless, superhero-like role models presented in the media. No wonder there is an increasing fear of being 'found out'.

Imposter Phenomenon

The 'imposter phenomenon'[2] describes persistent doubts of one's own skills and competence. It comes with feeling like a fraud, fear of failure, guiltily feeling undeserving of your success or 'luck', and a sense of dread about being exposed. This fear of not being 'good enough' can be sharpened in unfamiliar situations – a new course, promotion or career change. Ironically, successes such as an award, praise or promotion can add pressure and exacerbate the sense of feeling undeserving and less competent than others think[3]. People who have been seen as 'high flyers' and then experience a perceived failure, from a lost client to redundancy, or one of life's curveballs, can suddenly find themselves doubting their ability. Effects include reduced self-confidence which can impact upon wellbeing and performance.

An estimated 70%[4] of people will experience the imposter phenomenon, also known as imposterism, at least once in their lifetime. It is natural to experience insecurities and helpful to remember that you are not alone. Many public figures have shared their imposterism experiences; acclaimed writer Maya Angelou, New Zealand's Prime Minister Jacinda Ardern, award-winning actor and rapper Riz Ahmed and former US First Lady Michelle Obama have all spoken out. The more we talk about this common experience, the greater our chance of reducing the lonely sense of shame and countering its limiting power over us.

Leadership Vulnerability

Being a leader can take you into especially vulnerable places - the unfamiliar, high pressure and high visibility. There can be a burden of responsibility, with everyone looking to you for guidance in the big moments (wow, how I have felt the weight of that one!). The expectations of clients and shareholders, managing your team's needs and managing upwards, brings multiple demands. The pressure of 'the buck stops here', intense scrutiny and even perfectionism, can be a heavy mix. Organisational cultures such as a competitive, intensely target-driven or blame culture, can magnify our insecurities. Understandably doubts can creep in, including the echoes of past put-downs and the imposter phenomenon. Internalised oppression[5], where we absorb negative portrayals and stereotypes about our own identity, amplifies the inner critic. This often comes with the pressure to overwork, 'you have to work ten times harder to prove yourself'. But before we can dislodge negative self-talk we need to be able to observe it, to notice what that inner saboteur is saying.

Turning It Around: Identify The Doubts

For some people this may already be familiar; you may be acutely aware of your inner critic and where those limiting beliefs stem from. However, some people may find it difficult to identify the doubts and messages that have been absorbed. It can be subtle or something that we have become so accustomed to that we do not even notice it, like the air around us, until we take the time to really notice and question it.

Tuning In

When facilitating workshops some of the self-doubts most often shared with me by participants include:

'I'm not good / smart / popular / confident enough'

'I can't handle public speaking'

'I'm not ready for promotion'

'People won't listen to me / take me seriously'

'I'm too old / young / shy / clumsy / chatty / slow / forgetful'

'I can't do it'

'I'm a fraud'

'I'll make a fool of myself / people will laugh'

'I don't belong here'

'No-one else here / at that level looks like me'

'Wins like that don't happen for people like me'

'I'm hopeless at numbers / tech / reports / strategy / creativity / talking in meetings'

'I'm making it up as I go along'

These examples may help to spot what feels familiar for you or, if not, to appreciate that many people you work with do grapple with these worries. By the way, colleagues with those thoughts are often widely perceived as high performers by their peers and others.

If you are finding it challenging to identify your self-doubts, try these steps:

- Keep a journal, reflecting on each day, especially noting the thoughts you experience in moments of high pressure, visibility, new or uncomfortable situations

- Ask trusted friends and mentors for their observations on any fears, self-deprecation and insecurities you have expressed to them

- Challenge yourself to try something out of your comfort zone, or even to consider a hypothetical scenario that would feel daunting, and notice what thoughts come to mind

Why Are Thoughts Of Inadequacy Lingering In Our Minds?

Each person's inner self-talk will be unique to them, often shaped by early life experiences. A remark from a teacher, parent/ carer or bully, from the playground to the boardroom to an ex-partner, can stay with us, playing on repeat in the mind for years. Such instances accumulate into a record of criticism received, disappointments endured and perceived shortcomings listed. Like a terrible kind of stock-take, our mind can be a discouraging archive of all these negatives, which take more time and emotions to process and therefore take up more space. This leaves only a limited shelf available for the storage of praise and achievements[6]. The effect is compounded for anyone who has faced a deficit of affirmation, unhealthy relationships, hardship, and trauma. Oppression heightens self-doubts through experiences of low expectations and put-downs, discrimination, and dehumanising objectification. Day-to-day microaggressions build up; there is a cost to self-esteem when existing in a society (and workplace) in which people who look or live like you are rarely presented in a positive light, if represented at all[7].

Assess The Credibility Of The Source

It is not easy to dismantle these embedded notions, but the next step to unpick them is to assess the credibility of the source. Whether that is a specific person or a more general exposure to media and societal pressures, let's interrogate the source that is breeding self-doubts.

Useful questions include:

- Who planted that doubt and what was/could be their motivation?
- Was the source well informed or acting from assumptions, limited information, or bias?
- Is the source known to be a reliable one? For example, if the source is the media, it is well-known for bias; if it is a specific person, does it fit a wider pattern of behaviour?
- Even if that comment was valid at the time, is it still true today?

Challenge The Doubts

Would you like to be liberated from these feelings of inadequacy? Then it's time to take on that little liar living uninvited in your head. In the words of William Shakespeare, 'our doubts are traitors'. A turning point for me in my personal journey with shaking off the self-doubts was recognizing and naming the doubts as lies, not truths.

That doubting inner voice reflects the acronym: False Evidence Appearing Real (FEAR). So, how can we uproot the FEAR to free ourselves from self-sabotage?

- **Analyze the FEAR:** On a piece of paper, or on your device, note your self-doubts and then create two lists – 'evidence for' and 'evidence against'. Add facts to each list. Really challenge yourself to break down the doubt and seek examples from your experience to disprove it. Ask a friend or mentor to help you.

- **Choose self-care over FEAR:** Would you say such negative things to a friend? Unlikely. Identify the inner FEAR voice as a harsh, unreasonable liar and saboteur and choose instead to be a good friend to yourself. Do things that nourish you. Surround yourself with people who praise and encourage you. Seek a mentor and training opportunities to develop. Counselling, therapy, and affinity consciousness raising groups, can help to uproot entrenched internalized oppression and deep wounds to self-esteem[8].

- **Voice the FEAR:** Expressing the FEAR, instead of suppressing, lessens its power over you. Talk to a supportive friend who will affirm your strengths; this is especially helpful as we tend to focus on our perceived failings. Seek out support groups to talk with. The more we have honest discussions and hold space for our vulnerability[9] the more we will break down the private shame and suffering in society.

- **Re-write the FEAR:** You are the author of your own story; re-imagine the moments you received put-downs and change the script in your mind to praise instead. Try using realistic, positive, and encouraging language to re-write your doubts as beliefs. For example, 'I'm rubbish at speaking in meetings, I get so scared' might realistically be replaced with 'I speak well in meetings when I prepare in advance and the 'butterflies' (nervous feeling) in my stomach show that I care'.

- **Out-mantra the FEAR:** Tear up that list of self-doubts, take your replacement affirmations and display them on a mirror or turn them into a screen-saver; you could record yourself saying them and play it back as a daily meditation, or make them into a creative framed picture on the wall. Read them aloud daily. With practice and repetition, the new chosen self-belief is amplified. It may help to think of this exercise like playing music; you are turning down the volume on the song you no longer wish to hear and turning up the volume of the song that makes you want to dance.

- **Face the FEAR:** Exposure to our fears builds up reassuring experiences that lessen the power of the doubts; consider something that you were once completely new to or daunted by but that you can now do without undue worry. As the artist Vincent van Gogh said, 'If you hear a voice within you say you cannot paint, then by all means paint and that voice will be silenced'.

Keep A Balance

Resisting self-doubts takes us on a path towards positive self-esteem, confidence and liberation. However, it is helpful to remember that doubts can also appear to protect us from perceived dangers, arrogance and even delusional greatness; be kind to yourself, rather than critical, when you notice the doubts coming into your mind. Self-doubts can be useful to gently check-in and question ourselves to prevent rash and biased decisions; humility is a valuable leadership trait.

Re-cap

- Identify the doubts

- Challenge the doubts

- Keep things in balance

Moving Forwards

With daily practice over time, replacing the self-doubts with affirming beliefs, the transformation will come[10]. You will increasingly arrive at a place where you do not need the validation of others, free from the past put-downs which echoed in your mind, in a balance of self-awareness, you will simply approve of yourself. And a good leader with self-belief, and who nurtures it in everyone around them, is an inspiring one.

Exploring the tools in this chapter with your team, across your business, will yield results, unlocking new levels of trust, goodwill and previously unvoiced brave new ideas for business success. An assured workforce delivers; praise and valuable feedback is given and received with confidence and the positivity is felt by clients as a magnetic trusted brand.

References

1. Hoang, Q. (January 2013). The Impostor Phenomenon: Overcoming Internalized Barriers and Recognizing Achievements. The Vermont Connection.

2. Clance, P.; Imes, S. (1978). The Impostor Phenomenon in High Achieving Women: Dynamics and Therapeutic Intervention. Psychotherapy: Theory, Research & Practice.

3. Sakulku, J.; Alexander, J. (2011). The Impostor Phenomenon. International Journal of Behavioral Science.

4. Hoang, Q. (January 2013). The Impostor Phenomenon: Overcoming Internalized Barriers and Recognizing Achievements. The Vermont Connection.

5. Hoang, Q. (January 2013). The Impostor Phenomenon: Overcoming Internalized Barriers and Recognizing Achievements. The Vermont Connection.

6. Baumeister, R., Bratslavsky, E., Finkenauer, C., & Vohs, K. (2001). Bad is Stronger than Good. Review of General Psychology.

7. Cudd, A. (2006). Analyzing Oppression. Oxford University Press.

8. David, E. (2009). Internalized oppression, psychopathology, and cognitive-behavioral therapy among historically oppressed groups. Journal of Psychological Practice.

9. Brown, B. (2022). The Power of Vulnerability. Independently published.

10. Firestone, R.; Firestone, L.; Catlett, J. (2002). Conquer your critical inner voice: a revolutionary program to counter negative thoughts and live free from imagined limitations. New Harbinger Publications.

About Vanessa Boon

Vanessa Boon is a joyful disruptor and facilitator of courageous conversations. A graduate of the Chartered Institute of Personnel & Development, she combines over twenty years' specialist equity, diversity and inclusion (EDI) experience with decades of grassroots social justice activism. Re-energising this field with informed, creative, thought-provoking and uplifting consultancy interventions, she has a track record of engaging hearts and minds, equipping people with practical tools and delivering positive results. She coaches and empowers individuals and, collectively, whole organisations across the business, public service and community sectors, to disrupt limiting beliefs, biases, policies and norms. Her award-winning projects and EDI 'SWOT' (Strengths, Weaknesses, Opportunities, Threats) Analysis for client organisations have made a difference; her workshops are often described as refreshing, powerful, memorable and fun. A nurturing facilitator of liberation, including the globally acclaimed Springboard women's development programme, she sparks oppression-busting self-belief and awakens the inner change-maker, with inspiring ripple effects.

LinkedIn *https://www.linkedin.com/in/vanessaboon/*

MPI Learning *www.mpilearning.com*

Influence Without Authority

Susan Croft

Promise

You do not need a senior role in your organisation in order to influence others. This chapter will show you where your authority lies and how to empower your influencing skills.

Key Messages

- Differentiating between influence and persuasion

- Identifying the key skills in influence

- Framing your message and your argument

Why Influence Is Important

As we continue to transform into an interconnected, interdependent, global workplace, the ability to influence will matter more. That's because leaders can no longer lead solely by the power of authority or position. They need the power of influence - the ability to affect the actions, behaviour, opinions of others - to get things done, regardless of authority.

To be an effective influencer, you need both substance and style. Even with a solid foundation of credibility and confidence you still may fall short if you don't understand the interpersonal dynamics at play.

Effective influencing and communication skills are indispensable in today's organizations. Command and control structures have given way to less hierarchical, cross-team and partnership working where you get things done by inspiring and collaborating.

There are a range of strategies, skills, and tactics you need to influence

At work we may want to influence people to:

- Meet organizational targets (i.e. motivate them)

- Work better together and avoid conflict (i.e. build teams)

- Help us put our ideas into practice

- Understand and remember information that you communicate

- Think and behave in a particular way.

Notice that I have not used the word persuasion as a substitute for influence. There is a good reason for this – they are quite different skills.

Influence Is Not The Same As Persuasion

Some people think that influence and persuasion are the same, but I disagree with this. Influence is far more subtle and longer term than persuasion which tends to be more direct and short-term.

Here's an example:

- A manager *persuades* her team to adopt a new system for processing expense claims. They begrudgingly comply to avoid negative consequences.

- A different manager over a period of time *influences* her team to adopt the same system pointing out the benefits to them so they willingly comply.

From these examples we can see that persuasion is aligned to position power, whereas with influence you do not need power or authority.

The Influencing Hub

Let's take a look at figure below which identifies the skills that affect your influencing power.

Personal Brand: This speaks to the effect you have on others and how you are perceived. Perceptions are formed through your appearance, mannerisms, communication style and your values. As a useful exercise, write down at least five adjectives on how you would like to be perceived in the professionally. Ask several colleagues or your manager to suggest five adjectives that describe you. If they agree with your list, great, and if not put together a plan to work on making those your desired perceptions a reality.

Strategy: Your influencing strategy is important and you should be clear on your message and on the benefits to the other party. You need to understand both the 'WIIFM' factor – What's in it for me and the 'WIITM' – What is it to me, in other words, 'why should I care'? This is a key to effective influencing. People change behaviour when it is in their own best interests to do so. Framing is another construct of strategy and we will consider this later in the chapter.

Influencing Styles: We all have different styles and these may change according to the situation. One person may have multiple styles and can call upon a particular one to deal with a certain influencing scenario. There is an exercise at the end of this chapter which will help you identify your own style. One key point to remember is that no matter your style, you should always be authentic. People see through a false or contrived style and this will not contribute to your influencing effectiveness.

Skills: There are many you need to develop to be a powerful influencer: Communication, listening, negotiation and empathy, among others. A good influencer communicates with brevity and impact, listens actively, is empathetic to the other party's viewpoint and is able to tackle objections and push-back through good preparation and thoughtful judgment.

Understand and motivate others: In my experience I have noticed that effective influencers are quite intuitive and have a good understanding of human behaviour. They understand what makes people tick, are able to walk in their shoes and know the motivational trigger points for each individual. This kind of understanding comes with age, wisdom and experience, or by asking someone who knows the person well. It can also help to have a basic knowledge of psychology and personality preferences. There are plenty of books on this as well as short courses which might be helpful.

Cultural Awareness: We all live and work in a diverse society with people from different backgrounds, races, religions and life experiences. Being attuned to different cultures, especially if you travel for work or are part of a global team, is vital in building relationships and influencing others.

Framing

Framing is a useful construct in influence. By placing a frame round your argument or view point you are able to develop key messages, identify possible objections from different stakeholders and generally frame your argument. The framing effect is the idea that designing the way information is presented can influence and alter decision making and judgement about that information. Through the use of images, words, and by presenting a general context around the information presented we can influence how people think about that information. For example, a manager may wish to influence his team to sign up for presentation skills training. These courses run throughout the year and are self-selected. The manager may frame this influencing challenge by 1) identifying the WIIFM factor for employees, 2) identifying possible objections and developing arguments to counteract them, 3) signing up for the training himself and sharing key highlights, 4) discussing the benefit of professional development generally.

Principles Of Influence

One of the greatest thinkers in this area is author, Robert Cialdini *Influence: The Psychology of Persuasion* (1984). Cialdini found that influence is based on six fundamental principles. Those principles still hold today:

- Reciprocation: This trait is embodied in all human cultures and is one of the human characteristics that allow us to live as a society. People generally feel obliged to return favours offered to them.

- Commitment and Consistency: People have a general desire to appear consistent in their behaviour. Salespeople play on this desire by having a potential buyer an initial, small, commitment and then holding the buyer to that commitment later in the sales process.

- Social Proof: People generally look to other people similar to themselves when making decisions. This fundamental is particularly noticeable in situations of uncertainty or complexity.

- Liking: People are more likely to agree to offers from people whom they like and can relate to. These may include:

- Physical Attractiveness

    - People who are most like themselves

    - People who pay them compliments

    - People who make them laugh.

Authority: People often react in an automated fashion to commands from authority and even to symbols of power.

Scarcity: People tend to want things as they become less available. This fundamental understanding has encouraged advertisers to promote services as 'time-limited offers.'

In 2016, Cialdini proposed a seventh principle, which he called, the Unity Principle. The Unity Principle states that the more we identify ourselves with others, the more we are influenced by these others.

When was the last time you thought about how you changed minds, shaped opinions, move others to act? The ability to influence your boss, your peers, your staff or other key stakeholders is one of the essential skills for leaders at all levels.

Each of these styles can be effective, depending upon the situation and people involved. A common mistake is to use a one-size-fits-all approach. Remember that influencing is highly situational.

Three Steps To Increase Your Influence

1. Gain trust

Gaining your colleagues' trust puts you in a stronger position to influence them. When your team members trust you, they can rely on your ability to lead them. To gain their trust:

- Be honest
- Be dependable
- Be trustworthy

2. Network with others

Networking entails connecting with and forming relationships with people in your industry, perhaps on a professional networking site. A strong professional network can boost your credibility, encouraging others to pay attention to you. Depending on your expertise level, you might identify and attend networking events in your industry.

3. Give constructive feedback

Giving constructive feedback can demonstrate to colleagues that you have great ideas and want to help. Accepting criticism is also an important part of providing and receiving constructive feedback. Feedback is beneficial in the workplace, since it leads to personal and business growth.

Nudge Theory

A nudge rather than a shove makes it more likely that an individual will make a particular choice, or behave in a particular way, by altering the environment so that automatic cognitive processes are triggered to favour the desired outcome. An individual's behaviour is not always in alignment with their intentions. It is common knowledge that humans are not fully rational beings; that is, people will often do something that is not in their own self-interest, even when they are aware that their actions are not in their best interest.

The theory is well described in the book by Richard Thaler and Cass Sunstein – 'Nudge – Improving decisions about health, wealth and happiness'. The authors claim that nudging is a way to influencing behavior without sales coercion. The intervention must be easy to apply and cheap to avoid and should also have a positive intention. A simple example; Restaurants will offer the chocolate mint or two with their bill and frequently get higher tips as a result.

Final Word

In summary, the ability to influence others with purpose and integrity is a critical leadership skill and the important thing to remember is that you do not have to carry a fancy job title in order to influence effectively. Your influencing authority lies not in your position or seniority, but rather with you as a person – the trust you engender, your skill at communicating, the logic of your argument, the respect with which people hold you and your authenticity.

Influencing Styles Quiz

Please take a moment to complete this Influencing Styles Quiz. Give yourself one (1) point for each statement you *Agree* with:

Style 1	
I like the rough and tumble of debate	
I like to take the lead	
I am dedicated to achieving my objectives	
I can sometimes seem bossy	
I am a determined person who will sometimes use the power of my position to achieve my goals	
I don't suffer fools gladly	
TOTAL	

Style 2	
I often use humour and charm to make things work	
I help others to see the aims and objectives they have in common	
I am a good communicators	
I think my personality is one of my strongest assets in influencing	
I express my views vigorously and create an energised atmosphere which helps things go well	
I can sometimes inspire people	
TOTAL	

Style 3	
I will often win support by offering something in exchange	
I actively prefer win:win outcomes	
I am probably tactical rather than strategic	
I bargain to get what I need	
I will hold my position until others are prepared to compromise	
I am aware of the games people play, and like to be ready to deal with their ploys	
TOTAL	

Style 4

I like to be clear about aims, objectives and procedures	
I let people know immediately when they have not met my requirements	
I prefer to have transparent standards, so everyone knows where they are	
I like to take a step-by-step approach	
I believe that getting the process right can sometimes be as important as the outcome	
I feel strongly that it is best to play by the rules – for me that is linked to integrity.	
TOTAL	

Style 5

I prefer to be open, and make my views and desires known to others	
I challenge views I disagree with	
I am calm, reasonable and rational in my approach	
I will always be clear about my intentions and motives	
I am brief, clear and uncluttered in the way I express my opinions	
I am quick to set out my ideas	
TOTAL	

Style 6

I go out of my way to involve those who are not participating	
I defuse conflict, so that we can go forward	
I listen carefully	
I will often ask questions as a way of focusing on key issues	
I try to ensure the environment is right	
I tend to take a chairing role if there is no formal chair	
TOTAL	

Style 7

I put the needs of others before my own	
I always try to create harmony	
I don't like competitive situations: I'd rather give in gracefully!	
I prefer to listen to others rather than state my own preferences	
I like to keep myself open to other people's ideas	
My role is often to be the glue that holds a group together	
TOTAL	

Style 8

I will often suggest getting more information before reaching a decision	
I am often the person who names a problem	
I am level-headed, I have my feet firmly on the ground	
I don't like to be rushed into making a decision	
I am often the person who asks the difficult questions	
I am wary of people who want to be inspired and dream dreams, it is better to be realistic	
TOTAL	

Style 9

I like to hear what others have to say before putting forward my own views	
I like to build a rapport with others	
I prefer to share power	
I sometimes get frustrated when others fail to take responsibility	
I prefer to be open with information	
I like to work with others to find the right solution, even if that takes more time	
TOTAL	

Now add up your totals in each of the nine styles and write down your highest, second highest and least high.

Now, please check the style descriptions are below:

1. Forceful

People who prefer a forceful style tend to be dominant, or inspirationally so (they will often be 'shapers' in the Belbin team types). This style can be useful in emergencies, and where you need simply to gain compliance (e.g. health and safety). However, it is less effective long term in winning hearts and minds.

2. Charismatic

Charismatic people tend to be good communicators and natural leaders, they create a buzz about them, and others are keen to please them. They need to ensure that they have really taken people with them, and that the influence sticks, even when they are not around.

3. Negotiating

Negotiators like the give and take of bargaining, and feel a compromise is a fair outcome. Compromise can be useful when goals are not clear – however, equally, negotiators need to ensure that they don't compromise their principles and/or get out manoeuvred by opportunists.

4. Procedural

The safety zone for procedural influencers is to know exactly where they are, and to feel confident that there is some order to things (trade union negotiators can often be procedural influencers). However, sometimes influencing requires a leap in the dark – thinking outside the box to find unlikely solutions.

5. Assertive

Assertive influencers will be assertive about their needs and their objectives, and will state them with as little 'fudge' as possible. They can sometimes seem a little blunt.

6. Facilitative (acting as chair or facilitator)

Facilitative influencers will ensure they get the rhythms and environment right; they will often take a position that is 'above the fray'. Need to be careful that their position is not overlooked. This style is particularly effective when the facilitator uses the 'chair' role to synthesize and propose a way forward.

7. Accommodating

The accommodator makes everyone feel good. Can be useful when it is important to signal unselfishness to those you wish to get on-side. This is often a good role to have as part of a team of influencers. However, the accommodator can often miss opportunities to influence, by holding back his/her own views.

8. Reflective/cautious

The good side of the reflector is that he/she does not make hasty decisions and will often get intelligent, workable solutions to problems. However, their insistence on naming the problem can be seen as negative, and they can sometimes be perceived as lacking courage.

9. Collaborative

This approach is very valuable when you need long term, healthy relationships to reach well defined long term aims. It is democratic and when used well will bring out the best in others. However, it can be very time consuming and it assumes that everyone is equally committed to a partnership of equals and will take their fair share of responsibility.

About Susan Croft, BA, PMP, ATP

Susan is an international public speaker, corporate trainer, public relations practitioner and qualified executive coach. She is accredited by the Project Management Institute to teach project management courses and the PMP prep program. Susan is a Partner with a training consultancy where she is responsible for sales, communications, project management and leadership training. She was also a co-founder and Executive Director of a mobile learning company based in London that offers mobile learning and information solutions to business. She holds a BA from UCL and has a Post Grad diploma in executive coaching from Bristol Business School.

LinkedIn *https://www.linkedin.com/in/susan-croft-105600/*

MPI Learning *www.mpilearning.com*

Empathetic Leadership:
How To Enable (And Not Enforce)

Matthew Storey

Promise

You will connect with the certainty that your emotional intelligence must be exceptional to be an effective professional leader.

Key Messages

- How to readily identify your 'empathetic index' and how it dramatically influences your ability to lead

- How helping someone to uncover their hidden emotions is the key ingredient to great leadership

- How being an authentic and empathetic leader is even more important in the modern age

If the hidden emotions of every human being were superimposed onto a canvas, what images would be painted from their experiences of leader behaviour?

Since the global pandemic, the subject of human 'close contact' has been widely documented. This has been from a physical point of view – yet what about from a mental standpoint? When people had more time to think in isolation, their emotions simultaneously sharpened, and their senses heightened. They began to think much more about what was important to them mentally.

It was even more telling that such emotions had never been widely shared in the workplace.

Just before the pandemic hit, surveys revealed that a third (33%) of all UK workers will conceal their real emotions with 'a positive face' at work. It is therefore fascinating to disclose that after the pandemic, almost two-thirds (65%) of workers testified that working for an organisation with an empathetic and authentic leadership team has become more important to them. This is precisely why the empathetic leader is even more relevant in today's world.

The implications for all businesses are stark and clear: empathetic leaders are key to the retention of staff.

The inevitable business outcome of displaying a lack of empathy will be indisputable: surveys revealed that over half (58%) of UK employees would consider leaving their job if company leaders didn't show empathy.

Tellingly, 27% have already considered handing in their notice for this reason. The empathetic clock is ticking...

Therefore, how do you feel about this? How much do you think leader behaviour effects emotions? Have you suppressed your own emotions in the past when working with someone? How about recognising others' feelings whilst you have been a leader? Do you only spot the visible emotions? How would you even know that there are hidden emotions?

It is intriguing to add that over a third of staff (35%) previously felt that bravado and 'tough' leadership was more important pre-pandemic – but not now. Therefore, this is a real transition for many leaders, and we can all certainly empathise with that!

Therefore, let us take this moment to enable YOUR leader behaviour to take centre stage. In light of the above, one good litmus test of modern leadership can be offered:

Has the leader helped to uncover the hidden emotions of their followers?

That is why presenting the modern context of a 'contagious pandemic' is so compelling. Humankind has always lived in a 'social contagion,' where good (or bad) behaviours and emotions will spread spontaneously. The word 'spread' is used again for obvious reasons – like a physical pandemic, there are 'neural' pathways to our brain that connect the canvas of human emotion. This is the mental side of our behavioural-led world.

As a mindset and personal development coach that has mentored thousands of leaders in blue-chip companies across the globe, in addition to much smaller sized family businesses, it is clear that empathy is the answer to so many of these mental puzzles.

This is the 'emotional contagion' challenge.

How do we lead with our own beliefs (brightly displaying the positive ones), whilst also being aware of the hidden colours within somebody else's emotions? For example, how do we spot 'false' bravado? What is real and what is fake?

That is the role of an empathetic leader. To understand people and help them find their true path. The psychology of human interaction through sharing more emotions. Prior to Covid, a staggering 59% of UK workers have experienced emotions at work that they felt they could not freely express. That is why developing an empathetic response to these colleagues is so critical. This style of response will be to consider the positive intention of everyone around you. It means this - do you know WHY somebody does what they do through their eyes?

By understanding this – and then helping that person share such inner thoughts – that is showing empathetic leadership.

How can we show this today on a practical basis? What solutions are there? What tools can help us?

The psychologist Daniel Goleman popularised empathetic 'emotional intelligence' by highlighting the five key competencies needed for leaders to help their teams. These are self-awareness, self-regulation, motivation, social skills, and empathy itself.

Over the years, when coaching others, I developed this existing theory by adding an 'empathetic index,' which I used to help others develop their own empathetic journey. As you will see below, this spells out the word 'empathetic.' It is then linked to each of the five competencies of Goleman's model with TWO clear actions that leaders can take to measure their own progress.

The ten areas of the index are listed below for easy reference, with the emotional intelligence area in brackets.

Empowered (Self-Awareness)

Mindset (Self-Awareness)

Peace (Self-Regulation)

Acceptance (Self-Regulation)

Tact (Motivation)

Humanitarian (Motivation)

Engagement (Social Skills)

Trust (Social Skills)

Interpersonal (Empathy)

Compassion (Empathy)

This provides you with the practical knowledge that each of the ten areas function as your personal emotional 'checker.' It helps you sense your ability to find your own balance.

The framework itself means that you can score yourself out of ten for each area, which will add up to an index of one hundred. It is about ranking yourself each day – and knowing the scores will change for every day of your life. We are human! Transformational leadership (to make a lasting difference to other people) has its roots in really thinking about how you interact with others. As a daily habit! This can even be facilitated in a 'zen' like manner – so relax - the scores are yours only – and remember that it is just free information to help us all.

When you realise this, it makes any score out of one hundred relevant. This is because true perspective as a leader is seeing things from a fresh place every day. Until you can trust your own senses, you cannot influence fully as a leader.

Let us be clear – this is not an ego trip to get to a score of one hundred, as positive as that 'technically' is. It is about the process of being able to develop higher consciousness of what empathy is.

You become better in communicating as a leader – because you have empathetic values that are rooted in a greater understanding of yourself. It is then within your gift to help discover the hidden emotions of others – that litmus test of leadership.

Remember that as you continue to empathetically lead, you will enable others to positively develop through the natural way a contagion works.

Goleman himself made motivation of teams a key element of the emotional intelligence model and this was linked to having an infectious personality that enables your employees to really want to work with you.

Let us dive into the detail of the empathetic index:

We start with self-awareness, with the qualities needed of having an 'empowered mindset.' These are standalone qualities too – feeling empowered and having the right mindset – and both apply before you have even left your bed in the morning! Effective leader behaviour is helped by liking ourselves first. You cannot lead others if you are an enemy to yourself. We cannot 'fake' the other eight areas, without these first two, being in the right place.

Remember – everything is interlinked in the index.

Peace and acceptance are two integral qualities. It makes up the next stage of self-regulation. Empathy in leadership has so much to do with self-regulation. We need to consider how we can control OUR emotions, which will enable OTHERS to release theirs. This is such a key ingredient in transformational leadership!

Releasing hate and promoting peace is one of the biggest areas of the index. Many coachees have admitted that the ability to practice regulating their feelings to think of peace is a notable change for them. For example, 'softening' social media and only seeking to make positive comments on any news article is a fascinating skill to master – and an exciting one. You become a spreader of positivity as you only start see or hear positivity around you, through your actions as a leader. It is just like creating your own real-life algorithms!

Acceptance is then the natural by-product to such activity – by promoting peace, you become more accepting in what you control and accepting what you do not. It will begin to mark a wonderful change in behaviour in people around you too.

Motivation is the next section – and this is an ongoing way of life. Here are two questions for you: firstly, do you know how much your tact can change somebody's life? Tact is an emotional skill of Kings and Queens – look back into history - you can see when it is there and when it is not! Tact is a daily 'free gift' that we can bestow on the world. When you realise that, the motivation becomes unstoppable! Being 'humanitarian,' too, dovetails beautifully with this feeling. It will sound bizarre - yet talking to yourself in the mirror to say 'I want to be more humanitarian today' is so effective – because so many people never consider this. It also makes you smile with the realisation that YOU have the supreme power to change lives. This will be irrespective of money or status – just through influence. It is intuitive to say this repeatedly – 'influence is NOT money or status.'

'Engagement' and 'trust' are listed under the banner of social skills, as they only arise through skills-based behaviour in social settings. Put simply, trust is only earned – and returned – through one thing (and one thing only).

Consistency of values. Each time, every time.

Start to think about mistrust in personal relationships and Governments, for example. The two salient reasons will be a lack of values – or a clear inconsistency in 'displaying' them. When coaching this internally, ask one question – 'do you know what you stand for in the eyes of others?' What do you think they say about you to their network?

Engagement, meanwhile, is all about questions – seeking first to understand, before being understood. This is all about lighting a 'fire' in others – fresh questions, intuitive questions, questions of 'resonance' and evaluative questions. For example, asking 'when will you know that you will feel on track' and 'what will being 'on track' feel like'? What will you be saying to yourself when you are on track? Why do you even need to be on track? Your eyes and ears will tell you the questions to ask – trust your senses. It will help to unlock theirs! The question for you right now is – do you ask enough of these questions as a leader? Be critically honest when you rank yourself in the index.

Finally, empathy itself – to remind us that an empathetic leader is never finished! The words 'interpersonal' and 'compassion' are so empathetic. To be interpersonal is to build lasting relationships

– not just accomplishing tasks – so do you have a balance in this area? Compassion, too, is essential – do you speak to others with a beating heart, rather than just by way of an order? Ultimately, effective and empathetic energy will only be transferred if you genuinely care. This is true emotional contagion.

Leaders have told me that they have both uncovered and rediscovered their purpose through using these daily habits, within the index. In fact, I encourage the following activity for everyone reading this:

Look out of a window once a day, just by yourself, close your eyes and take ten minutes to work through the ten points of this index. Then, repeat the process every day!

The ultimate result? You will help people uncover their hidden colours, as well as finding out more about yourself as a leader!

To link back to the question posed at the start of the chapter, we can now constantly explore our feelings about that canvas of human emotion – are more images now emerging? Can we help them emerge with much more clarity?

That is empathetic leadership!

References

- Goleman, D, 1995: 'Emotional Intelligence: Why It Can Matter More Than IQ'

- https://www.totaljobs.com/advice/emotions-at-work - accessed 30.10

- Vitreous World, April 2021 'Workplace from Facebook' survey – accessed 30.10

About Matthew Storey

The empathetic 'transformation motivator,' Matthew passionately cares for the growth of others and has a unique memory for people and their needs. His focus has always been on facilitating the provision of an outstanding humanitarian experience and this led to his career into the field of training, coaching, and  mentoring across the globe. His talent in understanding leadership of the customer journey has seen him become a published author and his book 'The Three 'Rs' of Customer Service' continues to receive multiple outstanding reviews. He is a Master Practitioner in Neuro-Linguistic Programming and has developed award-winning leadership programmes.

When Matthew began his own company, his vision to empower others through learning began to reach a much wider audience. Since then, his work as a business trainer and qualified mindset coach has seen him train and develop thousands of people across the UK and overseas – across multiple industries.

Everybody speaks glowingly of Matthew's enthusiasm and passion for everything he does and his diligence and desire to coach others is second to none.

LinkedIn *www.linkedin.com/in/matthew-storey-a9694343*

MPILearning *www.mpilearning.com*

How Not To Be An Inclusive Leader

Vanessa Boon

Promise

Learn from specialist expertise alongside mistakes and pitfalls to avoid, plus adventures in self-discovery, tongue-in-cheek pointers and the collective learning from facilitating courageous conversations with thousands of people on this topic

Key Messages

- It all starts with self-awareness – or lack of it

- Deny, suppress and avoid a deep-dive into, those uncomfortable unconscious biases

- Embrace complacency and uphold the status quo – never mind all that *'inspirational leaders dismantle the systemic oppression that holds people back'* stuff, who wants to be a change-maker, anyway?

Inclusive leadership creates an environment where people can thrive and unlocks diverse talent for business success. Getting it wrong can be costly with damage to employee relations and wellbeing, plus the risk of litigation and embarrassing publicity.

The starting point for this work is always an exploration of what inclusive leadership looks, feels and sounds like, but people often find it easier to identify what it isn't, providing a valuable way into the subject.

It can be a useful exercise to approach a subject from the 'how not to do it' angle, not least because it often articulates a recognisable, all-too-familiar, experience which can clarify the pitfalls we wish to avoid, the different kind of leader we want to be, the transformation we wish to usher in. So, let's boldly jump in, employing irony as a tool to provoke thought, tongue-firmly-in-cheek…

Indulge In An Utter Lack Of Self-Awareness

Tales of the charmless insufferable boss have been told throughout the history of working life; reflected in popular culture, many novels and plays have featured the boss with no awareness of their flawed assumptions, awkward inappropriate remarks, and oblivious to, or uncaring about, their impact upon other people. Role models can be found in the pages of literary classics as well as the modern workplace sitcom and the mockumentary; the cartoon villain Mr Burns of The Simpsons, David Brent and Michael Scott in The Office, and the timeless Dickens' Ebenezer Scrooge all provide a template. More subtle examples can often be found in the workplace; consider which of the leaders you have worked with, and for, to draw inspiration from.

To excel in this area, it is necessary to avoid self-examination and models of interpersonal relations. Be warned, your colleagues in HR may attempt to engage you in these.

Among the models to be bypassed are:

- Betari's Box[1], illustrating the preconceptions one brings to an interaction and how they leak out through behaviour to flavour the relationship, like a self-fulfilling prophecy

- Johari's Window[2], shining a light upon gaps in self-awareness and authentic leadership

- I'm Ok, You're OK'[3] offering transactional analysis, mindful of power imbalances

Practical steps include making decisions and scheduling events without consulting, or considering the diverse needs of, participants and stakeholders. Choosing inaccessible and exclusive venues, digital platforms and methods, particularly those suited to one's own convenience are all well-established approaches. Nepotism, a scarceness of moral courage and insensitive communication alongside the evasion of compassion, humility and accountability can also be found among those eschewing inclusive leadership.

Be impervious to feedback, for example, about your conduct, biases, lack of allyship and your use of power. If you are invited to reflect upon microaggressions[4] or, worse still, to 'check your privilege'[5], embrace defensiveness and resist. These people are just leading you down a path of mind-blowing transformative self-knowledge and learning. Likewise for 360-degree appraisals, where one gains feedback not only from a supervisor but from various perspectives such as peers, employees, clients and diverse critical friends. Reverse-mentoring by a front-line worker with lived experience of oppression is to be dodged at all costs.

Steer clear of enablers of enriching self-discovery such as

coaching, reflective journalling, mindfulness, therapy, and the wide range of available psychometric profile tests to explore your personality, team role type and leadership style. Take no notice of people and approaches that 'hold a mirror up', inviting you to take a deep look at yourself, your attitudes, your behaviours and the source of your impressions about people living lives you have had limited exposure to.

Deny Any Possibility Of Having Unconscious Biases

Building upon the rejection of self-awareness further, one must avoid the uncomfortable deep-dive into unconscious biases[6]. If you don't know what is lurking in the depths of your subconscious mind, such as absorbed harmful stereotypes and othering, you can bask in being oblivious to the ways that your decisions may be weakened; for example, the ways you may automatically, unconsciously, judge people in a more positive or negative light, causing your decisions to be ill-informed, less fair, less objective. Ignore the warnings of inclusion champions highlighting how skewed decisions risk costly repercussions such as damage to wellbeing, goodwill and discretionary effort, talent retention, resourcing course-corrections, litigation and PR disasters.

There are several types of unconscious biases to relish in never examining yourself for:

- Affinity bias (liking people similar to oneself)

- Confirmation bias (powered by preconceptions, finding what we were looking for)

- Authority bias (giving more weight to the views of those with formal status and hierarchy power)

- Internalised bias[7] (absorbed stereotypes about one's own identity affecting self- and community esteem with potential for horizontal shared-identity discrimination)

- The 'halo and horns effect'[8] (the way that our quick first impressions cause us to view people in a more or less favourable light without basis in, and even contrary to, evidence)

- Groupthink[9] (the desire for harmony, consensus, conformity and avoiding conflict leads to poor decisions due to unexpressed differences or objections; going along with the group)

- In-group and out-group[10] dynamics ('them and us')

Regardless of the limiting effects that these biases can have on understanding your client base, effective wide-appeal service or product design, fair decision-making, unlocking the full talents of the people you work with, brand loyalty and business results – embracing denial and suppression is the way to go.

Unconscious biases are known to be especially influential when we make quick decisions[11] on 'auto-pilot', including when rushing or tired or hungry. Therefore, be sure not to take the time to give important matters deeper consideration and neglect the sort of self-care that enables you to draw conclusions when at your best; furthermore, stick with your own rushed assessment of people and situations without gaining other angles.

If you are encouraged to take the free online test that reveals your unconscious biases with recommended steps to mitigate bias, developed by researchers at collaborating universities including Harvard, known as the Implicit Association Test[12], you know what to do. Stay in your comfort zone.

Be A Champion Of Complacency And Maintaining The Status Quo

When the change-makers come knocking on your (non-open) door with fresh voices and new ideas, take a stand with the 'we've always done it this way' and 'if it ain't broke [for people who look or live like me], don't fix it' brigade.

Give critical thinking a wide berth. Take care to avoid discourse on intersectionality[13] (the way that the multiple layers of a person's identity, and associated types of discrimination, overlap and combine); the same goes for dismantling structural oppression[14] (embedded in institutions, hierarchies, policies and norms).

The shunning of approaches such as accessibility audits, co-production with diverse stakeholders, positive action to remedy past and persisting exclusion, and bold new ways to turn the company's stated inclusion values into meaningful action for improvement, all provide further illustrative blueprints for avoiding progress.

Assert that 'being equally polite to everyone' is enough. Be that person in the room who amplifies dominant voices and advocates for 'one size fits all' approaches. Be the torchbearer of the status quo. Neglect to consult people about their experience, needs and what would support them to thrive – go with your own assumptions, preferences and the way it's always been done.

Assume that you have sufficient, even superior, knowledge and skills for equality, diversity and inclusion – refuse further training and lifelong learning opportunities. Avoid new experiences that deepen insight and broaden horizons, reducing fear of the unknown and unfamiliar. Deny yourself the chance to experience the Human Library[15], where the diverse books are people and reading is an enlightening conversation with someone who has experienced stigma and stereotyping. Stick to books, films and events created by people who look and live like you do. Do not engage independent experts.

Deny the existence of institutional oppression[16] and systemic barriers embedded in policies and workplace norms. Instead, brag with confident certainty about the organisation being great on equality and diversity and how you've never heard of any discrimination or bias at work – especially if you are statistically least likely to experience discrimination yourself or so bigoted that no-one would ever approach you with a concern.

Finally, when voices of experience of exclusion speak up with feedback on what has gone wrong or how things might be done differently, don't listen to those who live it; reject humility, never acknowledge a faux pas, skip the emotional intelligence and instead employ denial and defensiveness. To really take privilege-fuelled fragility[17] (discomfort and defensiveness about inequalities that you do not face)[18] to another level, one might give those speaking up the career-limiting label of 'trouble-makers'.

Other classic moves include responding with vexatious counter-allegations and vengeful punitive measures using your power, e.g. appraisal, pay and promotion decisions, to make their lives more difficult; this breeds a compliant culture of fear, reducing the likelihood of further feedback and preventing change.

But Seriously...

It was not difficult to think of 'how *not* to' examples (and was quite cathartic) to write this wry piece. Sadly, it conveys the recurring themes from over two decades of dialogue, listening, training and facilitating in this space. However, it is joyful to support people to move from defensive folded arms to leaning-forward engaged positions, from confused and fearful to empowered. It is exciting to coach organisations on the journey to greater inclusion, helping everyone to get comfortable with the uncomfortable, to have those courageous conversations, and to see the difference that inclusive leadership can make.

Striving to be an inclusive leader takes on-going effort and yields inspiring rewards. It is important to acknowledge that we all make mistakes and we are all a lifelong 'work in progress'. It is likely that we will get it wrong sometimes (full disclosure: I've been there); we cannot be an expert in every circumstance, identity, culture, personality, every experience, every camera angle. However, it is how we take steps to be well-informed, proactively learning to design and nurture an inclusive workplace where everyone can thrive and celebrate both individual and collective 'wins'; it is our efforts to prevent adding to someone's mounting pile of drip-drip microaggressions endured, eroding their energy, self-esteem and wellbeing. It is the humility and compassion we can bring when we realise we have missed the point, said or done the wrong thing, left someone feeling overlooked or excluded, not safe to be their full self, or like they don't 'belong'. It is the sense and humility to listen to those who live it. It is the exciting potential to disrupt the practices that limit potential, limit lives and life chances. It is the opportunity to be a change-maker.

Enjoy the courageous journey ahead!

- Embark upon adventures of self-discovery and new experiences beyond the people most familiar to you

- Interrogate and mitigate against those unconscious biases

- Fight complacency and disrupt exclusive policies and norms – unleash your inner change-maker!

Reflective questions:

- Did you find anything familiar?

- Did anything feel uncomfortable or challenging to read, and why?

- Do you have any concerns or fears about 'getting it wrong' as you strive to be an inclusive leader? How could you address these concerns?

- What terms, models or concepts were unfamiliar to you, and why might these not have been on your radar?

- Are you curious to learn more about any of the terms and good practice approaches mentioned in this chapter?

- What support or training do you need to develop as a change-making inclusive leader?

- If this chapter provides a charter for how not to do it, what standards for inclusive leadership will you now set for yourself?

- How will you share what you have learned?

- What three steps could you take to cultivate inclusive leadership across your business?

References

1. Cotton, D. (2015). Key Management Development Models. Pearson.

2. Luft, J. (1955). The Johari window, a graphic model of interpersonal awareness. University of California.

3. Harris, T. (1967). I'm Ok - You're Ok. Harper & Row.

4. Cousins, S & Diamond, B. (2021). Making Sense of Microaggressions. Open Voices.

5. McIntosh, P. (1998). White Privilege and Male Privilege. Wellesley Center for Research on Women.

6. Banaji, M & Greenwald, T. (2010). Blindspot: Hidden Biases of Good People. Random House.

7. Clark, K & Clark, M. (1947). Racial identification and preference among Negro children. The Journal of Negro Education.

8. Thorndike, E. (1920). A constant error in psychological ratings. Colombia University.

9. Janis, I. (1973). Victims of Groupthink. Houghton Mifflin

10. Tajfel, H. (1970). Experiments in intergroup discrimination. Scientific American

11. Kahneman, D. (2012). Thinking, Fast and Slow. Penguin.

12. Greenwald, T & Banaji, M et al (1998) Implicit Association Test (IAT) - Project Implicit, Harvard University

13. Crenshaw, K. (1991). Mapping the Margins: Intersectionality, Identity Politics, and Violence against Women of Color. Stanford Law Review.

14. King, S. (2020). Make Change: How to Fight Injustice, Dismantle Systemic Oppression, and Own Our Future. DeyStrBks.

15. Human Library. (2022). https://humanlibrary.org

16. Macpherson, W. (1999). The Macpherson Report; The Inquiry Into The Matters Arising From The Death of Stephen Lawrence. UK Home Office Archive.

17. Eddo-Lodge, R. (2017). Why I'm No Longer Talking to White People About Race. Bloomsbury Circus.

18. DiAngelo, R. (2018). White Fragility: Why It's So Hard for White People to Talk About Racism. Beacon Press

About Vanessa Boon

Vanessa Boon is a joyful disruptor and facilitator of courageous conversations. A graduate of the Chartered Institute of Personnel & Development, she combines over twenty years' specialist equity, diversity and inclusion (EDI) experience with decades of grassroots social justice activism. Re-energising this field with informed, creative, thought-provoking and uplifting consultancy interventions, she has a track record of engaging hearts and minds, equipping people with practical tools and delivering positive results. She coaches and empowers individuals and, collectively, whole organisations across the business, public service and community sectors, to disrupt limiting beliefs, biases, policies and norms. Her award-winning projects and EDI 'SWOT' (Strengths, Weaknesses, Opportunities, Threats) Analysis for client organisations have made a difference; her workshops are often described as refreshing, powerful, memorable and fun. A nurturing facilitator of liberation, including the globally acclaimed Springboard women's development programme, she sparks oppression-busting self-belief and awakens the inner change-maker, with inspiring ripple effects.

LinkedIn *https://www.linkedin.com/in/vanessaboon/*

MPI Learning *www.mpilearning.com*

How To Become A Trusted Leader

Fraser Murray

The Promise

- Understand how to become a Trusted Leader and why character matters.

The Answer

- Character based leadership is the difference that makes the difference

- Adapt your style according to the situation and dial up the critical dimensions of character

Key Messages for senior leaders:

- The critical importance of character-based leadership

- The ability to develop and adapt your character strengths is differentiating

- Top tips to enable all your leaders and managers to become a trusted leader

I have been inspired by so many great resources, mentors and leaders in the last three decades. I would like to share some of the challenges and lessons that I've discovered whilst working as a global leader and coach on the ground in 34 countries. I hope these thought-provoking questions and tips can inspire those that want to become the best leader they can possibly be!

Character-Based Leadership

Most of us like to consider character as important during the recruitment phase. Do we really know what character is and how to select for it? Do we then follow through and invest sufficient time to help leaders sharpen these critical skills and personal attributes once on board? Probably not, but how much does it matter?

In my experience of three decades focused on training and coaching leadership, I have encountered hundreds of examples of leaders demonstrating key strengths but far too often those same strengths are overplayed and can create a culture of fear, leading to unethical decisions or sometimes people turning a blind eye to inappropriate behaviour.

Indeed, research based on recent court cases globally (see book reference 'Leadership On Trial) has shown how for example, the financial services crises was exacerbated, if not caused by a failure of senior managers to lead with the appropriate character for the situation.

In follow up research, building on the shoulders of giants in philosophy and psychology, Ivey Business School researchers conducted focus groups with hundreds of leaders and surveyed thousands to develop a framework of leader character based on ten separate dimensions that interact with an eleventh, the central quality of judgment.

Financial Services trials gave analysts a fantastic insight into the way varying leadership values and behaviours played out in various financial institutions across the world. Some organisations fared better than others. Why was that?

Research by Mary Crossan and the team at the Ivey Business School completely aligns with my own experience that leaders with exceptional character enable organisations to create significantly greater results. In my experience leaders who are humble and empowering, compassionate and caring, and who operate with values and integrity are hugely admired and respected. These are the type of leader people want to follow. They will choose to go the extra mile for them again and again.

These great leaders aren't just well-rounded personalities, their exceptional character comes through in their judgement and the decisions they make, leading to significantly better results for their teams, their organisations and their customers.

Too often senior leaders think in relation to good and balanced character that you either 'have it or you don't', without realising that these elements can be developed through high level training and one-to-one coaching.

Many senior leaders have high technical competence built on decades of experience. Many leaders accept that they have specific strengths and some underdeveloped aspects of character. It's become common to replace the word 'weaknesses' by calling such shortfalls 'development areas'.

However, how many leaders invest the necessary time to seek support to develop these areas? Do you?

In my experience only those with a deep desire to improve, invest in developing themselves fully.

Assessing And Developing Your Character

It is no longer considered acceptable for leaders to continue without tackling these 'development areas'. You need to strengthen in all dimensions of character, or what could be a strength will operate like a vice. Very few leaders recognize that what they thought was a strength is undermining their leadership. For example, what they thought was being principled is actually being dogmatic when they lack the humility and humanity to support it. You need to be able to dial up the critical dimensions of character in line with any situation you are facing. On occasions, where leaders have overplayed strengths, it might be necessary to balance potentially overplayed strengths such as courage and drive. Getting our judgement and decisions right in the critical moments is most important as the impact of success or failure on organisations and their people can be huge. One of the global clients I work with calls these the 'Moments that Matter'. How is your character in the moments that matter?

All the critical leadership behaviours and in particular dimensions of character can be a positive if applied appropriately within the context of the situation. However, some characteristics if displayed in excess or in the wrong situation, can be considered 'overplayed strengths' and can make the situation worse! Unlike other leadership development models which focus on strengths, character-based leadership emphasizes how if someone has an overplayed strength, that rather than 'dialing down a strength' instead, they should dial up a weaker area to help return the strength to a virtuous state.

Do you occasionally overplay one of your strengths? Do you invest in a coach to help you rebalance your character?

The secret is to be brilliant at all key dimensions and to dial them up, as each situation requires. I highly recommend all leaders to read 'Developing Leadership Character' as the complexities of each character dimension and the impact of their relationship to each other are clear in this excellent piece of research.

Have you ever watched a successful sports team and wondered what makes them so successful? Yes, they will often have skillful players, but many teams have talented individuals. Has your team ever won a major tournament or managed to stave off relegation on the last day of the season? If they did, how important was the 'character' of the individuals in your team?

Often 'character' can be the difference that makes the difference. Under immense pressure, those that win through are often those that show the perfect balance of calmness and composure, confidence and collaboration, creativity and courage.

Top Tips To Become A Trusted Leader

As Crossan and colleagues point out, trust is ultimately a character-based phenomenon – we trust people's judgment. Stephen Covey asserts that trust requires both character and capability[1]. Becoming that trusted leader is not easy. It does take character to develop character. This is a key difference with the Leader Character framework compared to other leadership models which do not give these matters such a priority but which my experience and research shows are of equal importance in how effective a leader is.

Switch Your Brain From Saboteurs To Sage

I was fortunate enough to learn from the great, Shirzad Chamine whose methodology highlighted many aspects that I found applicable in my work with senior leaders. Staying calm, not being sidetracked by your saboteurs, turning to the positive sage/wisdom side of your brain and thinking how you can calmly handle any situation at your best. You can't really do any better than that can you... other than to invest in your self-development so your 'personal best' is in future at an even higher performance level. Usually, I find this is achieved through a combination of both improved competence and character.

Feedback, Feedback, Feedback.
Become A Feedback Champion!

Great leaders are always open to learning and adapting. They regularly seek feedback on what they are doing well and what they could do even better. Then they implement anything that will help them raise their game to an even higher level.

Catch the feedback and accept their perspective. Stay calm and reflect on the feedback before you decide how to respond.

Remember even people who are poor performers or who don't like you, might have some useful observations so it's important to stay open minded to feedback from anyone!

Consider All Perspectives

Disagreements usually involve at least two different perspectives on the same issue. Instead of fighting to prove we are right, the trusted leader will endeavour to understand the perspectives of all the other key stakeholders. Why do they perceive things the way they do? What could I learn from putting myself in their shoes and truly understanding their perspective on the issue. Holding back in judging others until you've proactively sought everyone's perspective is likely to increase trust in these key relationships.

Hold Your Position Lightly

You may have a different perspective than others and you may well be right. However trusted leaders tend to be able to flex their position as circumstances and/or evidence changes. The easiest way to do this is to hold your position lightly and be prepared to adapt if necessary. If you are too definite in your views, the chances are you might miss something useful when considering the perspectives of others. Always keep an open mind and listen deeply to alternative views.

Meet People Where They Are At And Choose To Really Care

When hearing the views and feelings of others, the Trusted Leader accepts that it's ok for people to feel the way they do. Rather than judge others, it's best to seek to understand why they feel the way they do. All parties can then work together to resolve different perspectives, provided they too can keep an open mind and communicate effectively, considering the other person's experiences, feelings and viewpoint

People Will Almost Always Do The Right Thing, Given The Way They See The World

As an executive coach working globally with senior leaders and teams, one thing I've noticed over several decades is that people will almost always do the right thing ... given the way they see the world!

So, our job is not necessarily to tell them what to do, then give them feedback on what they did right or wrong, but rather to help them to see the world differently. We need to ignite their passion, support them with training and coaching, enabling us to trust them with more freedom and empowerment. If we can help them to see the world differently, they will make the right decisions and do the right things. They will choose to look after themselves, their colleagues and their customers. They will choose to lead with strong values, act with integrity, trim costs, grow profits and create innovative solutions.

They will deliver exceptional products and services, with care and compassion. They will lead with character and adapt to the situation.

By doing this, individuals will have even better motivation and a stronger connection between the vision and the team goals, all the way through to their individual objectives

Finally, the Trusted Leader recognises themselves and others are imperfect. We all make mistakes. When giving feedback in such situations always remember to recognise the positives and the intent first, before recommending future focused improvements. View failures as learning opportunities. Don't become known as someone who always criticizes others. Try to catch someone doing something right and if necessary, help (coach/train) them to do it better. Don't just point out their mistakes. Use your phone to schedule reminders to do positive acts if you need reminding, until it becomes just part of your natural style.

What Can You Do To Become A Trusted Leader And Drive Your Career Forward?

Last week, I completed a six-month coaching program with an

aspiring Trusted Leader. David works at a global consulting firm and is 90% of the way there already. He aspires to become global COO and I'm confident he will achieve it. He's his own biggest critic and very self-aware, with a desire to improve his control of his own mindset and emotions. He is usually very composed but occasionally, especially when run down, he can get frustrated and might let those feelings leak.

His self-awareness and desire to become even better are the first signs of him having real high potential. He already leads with great character and delivers bottom line results by keeping people on board and making things happen.

Is there anything you can learn from how David took ownership of his career and how he demonstrated many of the key character traits in the model to try to become the Trusted Leader. Here's what I observed David did after deciding to get a coach to support him:

1. Developed a clear career vision, including potential options and next steps (Transcendence) and took responsibility for making it happen (Accountability)

2. Considered his career plan in conjunction with his life plan, including partner and family in key decisions (Humanity)

3. Aligned his career goals to business strategy, structure and processes (Transcendence)

4. Built critical relationships with key decision makers (Collaboration)

5. Developed his existing team to cope without him when he was ready to move on (Courage) whilst inspiring, motivating and recognizing others consistently (Justice)

6. Improved his mental health, mindset, communicated transparently and authentically (Integrity)

7. Learned to manage his own emotions even better than before, choosing to be ok with rejection and believed he would succeed (Temperance)

8. Led with character, balancing achievement of results with doing it in his best style (Humility)

9. Became both calm and pragmatic to manage any situation 'at my best' (Temperance)

10. Got a significant promotion to his ideal next role, as part of his long-term career plan (Drive)

Hopefully David's role model behaviours will inspire you to take ownership of your career as you continue to maximize your potential.

Finally, my aim has been to enable you to become the Trusted Leader by helping you to understand what to focus on and why. If you want more help with the HOW, there are books, podcasts, webinars, and video clips out there to help you to learn and adapt. I also recommend you get yourself an internal mentor and an external coach, at any stage in your career where you recognise you might benefit from support to be the best leader you can possibly become! If you need help to find your ideal coach, see the Next Steps at the back of the book. Meanwhile very best of luck in achieving your potential. With the right focus and support you know you can become the Trusted Leader.

References

1. M. Crossan, G. Seijts, J. Gandz. 'Leadership on Trial: A Manifesto for Leadership Development' (London, Ontario: Ivey Business School, 2010)

2. Crossan, M.; Seijts, G; Gandz, J.; Developing Leadership Character, Routledge, 2016

3. Stephen M.R. Covey: The Speed of Trust: The One Thing that Changes Everything. 2006 Simon & Schuster UK

4. Crossan, M.; Byrne, A.; Seijts, G. Reno, M.; Monzani, L., Gandz, J.: 'Toward a Framework of Leader Character in Organizations' Journal of Management Studies, vol. 54 (7) 986-1018, January, 2017

About Fraser Murray

Fraser is a specialist facilitator and coach. He helps leaders globally to become Trusted Leaders by their organisations.

He utilises extensive research of thousands of leaders to help people assess and develop their leadership character.

Fraser's experience and expertise on leading change enables him to coach senior leaders through major challenges so they can more effectively manage the transition for themselves and their teams.

Although he has deep experience in financial services, Fraser has supported leaders in many organisations including HSBC, ANZ, ABN Ambro, RBS, Barclays, Deutsche Bank, State Street, Nomura, Mizuho, La Salle, National Australia Bank, Standard Life, Moody's, AXA Rosenberg, Evercore, ECM, Allied Domeqc, Heinz and University of Edinburgh.

LinkedIn *www.linkedin.com/in/frasermurray*

MPI Learning *www.mpilearning.com*

Next Steps

Angela Armstrong PhD

Summary

As I mentioned in Welcome, we sought to bring you a carefully curated selection of articles to save you re-inventing the wheel, making the same mistakes, or having to read gigabytes worth of e-books. We hope that you have been stimulated by the articles and that they have prompted reflection on your leadership style or those of leaders you are responsible for nurturing.

We selected articles about leading at three levels: leading the system, leading others to achieve business outcomes, and leading yourself.

Leading The System

The first few chapters provided insight into the current context in which leaders are tasked with directing, inspiring, and influencing employees, that a collaborative and collective leadership style is most effective. That leadership is 20% science and 80% art, requiring a high degree of understanding about human behaviour both as individuals and in groups.

That companies who set out to make 'profit on purpose' and that are intentional about creating a purpose-aligned company culture can expect to outperform companies focused on profit alone. Three priorities to succeed at culture transformation (coherence, consistency, and pace). We showed that talent is not scarce, and that you can find and liberate talent that is currently hidden in your organisation.

Leading Others To Achieve Business Outcomes

We shared five articles about maximising the talented people around you by creating a place where people love to work, where they thrive, stay, and attract more talent to you. We discussed psychological safety and how it sets the stage for constructive critique to achieve the best outcomes. In a similar vein, we looked at the skills and awareness necessary to become a more inclusive leader so that everyone feels able to fully contribute and belong. Having healthy interpersonal dynamics is only part of the picture, leaders also need to provide clear and concise outcome-led instructions to unleash initiative and drive accountability throughout the organisation. We also discussed providing future leaders the opportunity to develop their leadership skills through the practice of building and maintaining a high performing team.

Leading Yourself

To lead others requires that we first lead ourselves, which requires a great deal of self-awareness, emotional intelligence, and the ability to tune our character strengths to the situation at hand. Techniques for taking control of our own minds enable us to turn self-doubt into self-belief and enables us to unlock our full potential. Being able to demonstrate empathy, become a trusted leader and influence others without authority in the 'moments that matter', enables us to act with integrity and achieve aspirational business outcomes far beyond the capacity and capability of our direct reports. We also took a slightly tongue-in-cheek discovery trip on how not to be an inclusive leader! Just because we take our responsibilities as leaders seriously, doesn't mean we always have to be serious. After all, neuroscience has proven that we learn more when we play.

This book is just the tip of the iceberg in terms of our inhouse expertise on leadership development (90 learning professionals) and cultural transformation (60 learning professionals), but we hope you've learned something. Please use these questions to reflect on what you've read, and prompt actionable insights for you and your organisation.

- Which articles resonated most with you? What were your key take-aways?

- Describe the culture at your organisation? What works well? What would you change?

- Where can you liberate more of the talent that is currently lying dormant?

- Where does your organisation already have strengths in leadership succession? What's missing or in short supply?

- What will you do differently tomorrow as a result of what you've learned?

Get In Touch

We live in fast-changing times; intentionally developing a culture of lifelong learning is an investment that will continue paying dividends.

Partnering with MPI Learning is a bold and vital decision to deliver the organisational culture that differentiates your company and provides an unassailable competitive advantage.

For individuals, we offer world-class executive and performance coaching, live online learning modules and on demand digital learning. We also periodically post articles in the learning lounge on our website, and social media channels.

For organisations, we offer tailored, and bespoke, leadership development programmes. We're able to do it all for you, or work with your colleagues and other suppliers as necessary to deliver a programme that delivers your measurable business outcomes. We can also provide specialist leadership development modules to complement your existing arrangements, and world-class executive, performance, and team coaching. We also deliver UpAGear, our flagship 12-month Team Performance Programme, underpinned by uOnline (online process and methodology).

Don't just take our word for it, we're happy to provide additional case studies, testimonials, and pre-qualified access to senior clients.

If you want to find out more, we'd love to talk to you, please get in touch.

Our contact details are available at

https://mpilearning.com/contact-us/

About MPI Learning

MPI Learning is an international business learning and development provider, we are committed to improving the world of work by supporting individuals and organisations to maximise their performance and impact on society. We create learning experiences and environments that provide you and your people with the workplace tools needed to succeed in today's ever-changing marketplace. Working with us will help you embed lifelong learning as a core part of your culture.

www.mpilearning.com

https://mpilearning.com/contact-us/